1/20

"If you or someone you love is caught in addiction or is in the process of recovery, this is a must-read book! With gut-level honesty, Deborah and David Beddoe share their story—their failures and successes—and their passionate desire to help you find the answers you desperately seek. Not only is this book a compelling read, it's filled with specific information, techniques, and services, along with additional medical, emotional, and spiritual resources. Every person in ministry leadership needs this book, too!"

Carol Kent, speaker and author of *Staying Power*

"As a recovering addict myself, I know that healing and restoration for the addict and everyone around them can seem impossible. Deb and Dave's life is a picture of the impossible becoming possible. They've turned their experience into a manual for what real compassion and grace look like in an addict's recovery. How do you love when there's been so much long-term failure, damage, and broken promises? Deb and Dave show you how to genuinely care in your marriage, family, friendships, and community."

Gary Morland, author of *A Family Shaped by Grace*

"I have known this couple for over thirty years, and *The Heart of Recovery* is a great toolbox for informing family, friends, church leaders, or even employers how to identify and respond to the signs of opioid addiction. Forged from the fire of personal experience, this book exposes the reader to the practical issues and personal pain of recovery from a variety of perspectives. It is a MUST-READ for anyone involved in pastoral care. I will certainly use it as a resource for my Celebrate Recovery leaders."

Mike Kildal, executive pastor, Redeemer's
Fellowship, Roseburg, OR

"Deborah and David Beddoe have written an insightful and extremely helpful book, not only for people overcoming addiction, but also for family and friends who are profoundly affected as well and wish to offer truly helpful support. The Beddoes' personal candor, grace, broad insight, and practical wisdom are not to be missed."

Ron Friesen, spiritual director and director of LifePath, the recovery ministry of Salem Alliance Church, Salem, OR

"*The Heart of Recovery* provides a *flood* of hope for individuals and families crushed by addiction. Deb and Dave are living proof of the miracle of restoration. As the leader of a local church, I recognize that patterns of judgment and shame have only forced addicts into silent destruction. This book calls us to follow the heart of Jesus by allowing him to shape us into a community of grace, hope, and healing."

Jim Walter, pastor of Restore Church, Poulsbo, WA

"*The Heart of Recovery* is the loving but poignant wakeup call Christians need to no longer fear, hide, and avoid the world of addiction and recovery. Dave and Deb's story is raw, powerful, but most of all full of hope. Through addiction, homelessness, the long and messy journey of recovery, and everything in between—their story, captured in *The Heart of Recovery,* is proof that there is no brokenness or hidden shame that the Lord cannot redeem. This book has the ability to change the way we view addiction and recovery, and perhaps remove the shame and fear of those addicts and their families who are still suffering in silence. It is a must-read—not just for loved ones of addicts, but for all Christians—as each of us know someone—openly or still hidden—who is battling opioid addiction. You will cry, learn, be challenged, and most of all be encouraged that no matter the circumstance—with Jesus, there is always hope."

Kari Trent Stageberg, coauthor of *The Blessing* and host of The Blessing podcast

"*The Heart of Recovery* was like sitting with a dear friend and watching a home movie from a season of their life I had no idea they faced. Shockingly, this relieved me and saddened me. . . . How would I have responded had I known? Would I have caused more hurt or inspired hope? The expression 'You don't know what you don't know' clearly states that each of our perspectives are limited. No one person can know or understand everything. Ignorance, and even innocent good intentions, can cause more harm than good. The Beddoes open up a window into the beautiful and uncomfortable ways recovery can be accomplished, both for the addict and the loved ones surrounding them. *The Heart of Recovery* is a wakeup call (to both the church and health workers) that addicts live in tension between experiences of deep shame and healing compassion and that there is a vast chasm between immediate healing and the holy pilgrimage of recovery which addicts travel. We can walk with them."

Melinda Gray, RN, emergency room and surgical nurse liaison

"The Beddoes show that there are no formulas. Every recovery journey is as unique as every addict. *The Heart of Recovery* provided me with much needed encouragement to walk alongside my child with compassion and grace, embracing my own vulnerability and laying down my expectations. There have been no quick fixes—just God's love flowing through me to love my addicted child and show them they are not alone."

Anonymous, mother of a heroin addict

"Deb and Dave Beddoe have been given the truth and are speaking it through the authority found in living, surviving, recovering, and enduring addiction."

Anonymous, wife to a husband recovering from addiction

THE HEART OF
RECOVERY

THE HEART OF
RECOVERY

How COMPASSION and COMMUNITY Offer Hope in the Wake of Addiction

DEBORAH and DAVID
BEDDOE

Revell

a division of Baker Publishing Group
Grand Rapids, Michigan

Published by Revell
a division of Baker Publishing Group
PO Box 6287, Grand Rapids, MI 49516-6287
www.revellbooks.com

Printed in the United States of America

Library of Congress Cataloging-in-Publication Data
Names: Beddoe, Deborah, 1969– author.
Title: The heart of recovery : how compassion and community offer hope in the wake of addiction / Deborah Beddoe and David Beddoe.
Description: Grand Rapids : Revell, a division of Baker Publishing Group, 2019. | Includes bibliographical references.
Identifiers: LCCN 2019007006 | ISBN 9780800736552 (pbk.)
Subjects: LCSH: Church work with recovering addicts. | Church work with drug addicts. | Church work with medication abusers. | Substance abuse—Religious aspects—Christianity.
Classification: LCC BV4460.3 .B43 2019 | DDC 248.8/629—dc23
LC record available at https://lccn.loc.gov/2019007006

Deborah Beddoe is represented by the William K. Jensen Literary Agency.

The names and details of the people and situations described in this book have been changed or presented in composite form in order to ensure the privacy of those with whom the author has worked.

Contents

For our families, friends, and community
that never let go.

. . . .

We are lost unless we can recover compassion,
without which we will never understand charity.
We must find, once more, community,
a sense of family, of belonging to each other.

MADELEINE L'ENGLE

Introduction

Years ago, someone told me the best way to tell our story would be to write it together. Dave and I both balked at the idea. I'm the writer, he's the talker. I wanted to dig deep into our past, consulting journal entries for accuracy, while Dave—who has very little filter anymore when talking about his addiction and recovery—wasn't too thrilled about wandering back through the sordid details.

Conversations with people in desperate circumstances with their loved ones revived an idea we'd had early in his recovery. We believed our experiences with prescription drug addiction were just a prelude to what the community, church, and nation were about to face. Fifteen years of addiction took a terrible toll on each of us, our marriage, family, and ministry. But our personal experiences with the opioid crisis demolished and rebuilt our understanding of grace, leaving us insight into the world of addiction and recovery that we would never have had, had we not been through it ourselves.

Ours is not a street drug story. Our homelessness didn't mean sleeping in a car. Our story is about hidden addictions that destroy lives. It's about the shame we felt as people who had a problem that "good people" don't have—certainly not Christians. We were in full-time ministry. We "didn't belong" in the welfare office, or in rehab in a state hospital, or in weekly 12 Step meetings.

Over the years, I believed a lot of lies about addiction—even while we were living in it. The most powerful one was that we had to keep it a secret. Our lives began to change dramatically when we allowed people into our shame and pain. Through the years, that shame and pain has been healed by God in the context of community: in our family, in our friendships, in our ministry, and in our small town.

Rather than leaving the opioid addiction epidemic to slow legislation and a shortage of recovery professionals, we need a church that is educated and unafraid. We want to encourage you with hope, stir your heart to compassion, and persuade you to step toward people working through the recovery process as well as those who are still trapped in addiction. To these people, the situation can feel hopeless. Our intent within these pages is, to give you much-needed support as you walk beside a loved one in recovery.

As a culture and as a church, we've taken *we can't change people* to mean *people don't change.* And we've taken *we can't change people* to mean *there's nothing we can do to help them change.* But when we buy the idea that people don't change, we deny both the human capacity for change and the power of God to change the human heart. And maybe, most tragic of all, we free ourselves of the discomfort of close relationship with someone who needs us, effectively abandoning the mission God has set right in front of us.

Grace allows time and space for transformation. People do change. People consumed by addiction can recover. Marriages can be saved. Children can survive dysfunctional homes. But it's a process. We forget this. It doesn't happen overnight. Recovery takes endurance.

Dave has been clean now for more than a decade, and though we celebrate his recovery, it hasn't been easy. The addiction years were a trauma of their own: we sank deep into a pit trying to fight addiction alone. But the recovery years have been a long haul of living "one moment at a time," taking slow steps in the right direction, getting knocked down, and being pulled to our feet again by each other and the willing bystanders in our lives. If the strength and power of the years of addiction was secrecy, shame, and darkness, the power of the recovery years has been transparency, love, and community.

—H DAVE—

Eight years ago, Deb started writing online about our journey through addiction and recovery as Christians, and we sat down to reflect on the questions that had poured in. At the time, very few Christians were talking publicly about prescription drug addiction, but we believed that at some point, the dam would break on this issue like it had for us. I was sure there were other Christians struggling with pills.

We gladly shared hope and practical advice with anyone who asked. We discussed the conversations we'd had with teachers, medical professionals, and even law enforcement about prescription drug addiction. We wrote out as many answers as we could from our own fresh experience with recovery and restoration. But we didn't know at the time if what "worked" for us would work for other people. I was only three years clean myself, we had just started a recovery program in our church, and we still had a lot to learn. And frankly, we didn't even know if I'd be able to stay clean.

Part of the power of a secret addiction is the shame and pride and fear that stop you from confessing your need for help. For fifteen years, I'd let no one into my battle unless I was caught. When it all came out, I had a weird mix of terror and numbness and relief. I had been so sure that Deb would leave me and that everyone would hate me. I'd hidden my addiction through years of ministry, so naturally there were people in my life who were shocked, hurt, and angry. But the overwhelming response I got was not what I expected. I expected condemnation, and instead I received compassion. Once I let people in to help, I discovered that a supportive environment can make all the difference not only in getting clean but for sustained freedom from addiction.

Whenever I tell my story of overcoming addiction, people comment on the strong relationships I had and remind me that not every addict has that kind of support. I know they're right. I'm forever grateful that in spite of the disappointment and pain I gave the people in my life, some of them stuck around to give me one more chance, hoping that maybe this time my healing was the real deal.

But even in my story, "support" didn't always look or feel like the support we wanted or thought we needed. For many people I knew, I was their first experience dealing with an addict up close.

Addicts burn a lot of bridges, and I was no exception. I know I was written off by some people because of the guy I was when they knew me. It happens when you fail too many times. We're a *three strikes and you're out* kind of culture, and we have been for a long time now. And if you wear through every strand of the safety net, when you finally fall for good, there's no one left to catch you.

I wish I could say to those people, *the church will be there for you.* But church is often the last place a broken person feels welcome. And I think it's often harder for the Christian community to offer compassion to someone who's been given so many chances and failed.

The community that caught my family and me when I fell wasn't made up of a perfect pastor, family, or church that had it all figured out. Our safety net was held by people who were willing to respond with compassion and reexamine what they thought they knew about addiction and addicts and this idea of "recovery." Family and friends who wrestled intensely with forgiveness and continued to try to love an addict, even when he broke their hearts. A wife who was willing to practice the countercultural idea of forgiving seventy times seven.[1] And a broader community of broken people who welcomed me as a brother. *The Heart of Recovery* is a testimony of the power of God working through compassion and community to transform us.

After more than a decade free from pills, we can simply say with confidence, here's how we got this far: people around me set aside their fears, prejudices, and objections and stepped into my life to help. Hope began in community through the compassion of a group of bystanders who were willing to move past the stink of our lives and do what they could to help.

———— ⊞ ————

Dave and I are not counselors or therapists, and we ask that you view this book in that light. But we can tell you what made it possible for me to stay in our marriage and for Dave to remain in recovery. We would also urge you to seek help from a qualified professional if you are in an abusive situation.

People in addiction recovery may find some hope in our story, but we have written this book with those around them in mind. As you read, we hope you'll gain a better understanding of the consuming and destructive power of prescription opioids and the urgency to act in this present crisis.

We pray that you will see your place in the story of healing. That you'll find challenge, comfort, and encouragement—whether as the spouse of someone in recovery, their parent, pastor, or friend—and that you find others around you who are going through recovery beside a loved one as well.

And that, along with the help this book will provide, you will also find community.

one

Shame Buries Us

> If we conceal our wounds out of fear and shame, our inner darkness can neither be illuminated nor become a light for others.
>
> BRENNAN MANNING

The morning news reminds us again of the miracle that Dave is alive and free from the addiction that had a hold on him for fifteen years. Today, another great musician died of an overdose. Last week, an actor. And in between the Hollywood headlines are the local ones, closer to home, more personal and, tragically, more and more often.

Over eleven million Americans have abused prescription pain-killers in the past year, and according to the Substance Abuse and Mental Health Services Administration, 1.7 million of us struggle with addiction to them.[1] As of this writing, prescription drug overdose is now the leading cause of death for Americans under the age of fifty.[2] The opioid crisis has invaded our communities and our homes, and the quest for solutions has become a billion-dollar industry.[3]

Addiction and overdose are tragic side effects of the collision between the War on Drugs and the War on Pain. It's a mess of our own making, and we have tried and failed to fix it at the highest levels of government. Generation X grew up with Nancy Reagan's *Just Say No* campaign to keep us from turning to drugs when we were teens. And then, in the 1990s, as we were becoming adults, Jack Kevorkian gave the moral compass of the country a spin with his assisted suicides for people who were suffering unquenchable pain.[4] The American public, appalled by euthanasia, pushed lawmakers to stop it.

Under pressure and caught in a dilemma, Congress held special sessions to hear testimonies from pain sufferers and their family members as well as arguments for pain relief from physicians. The result was a decision that would change modern medicine: *We can't let people live in pain. Stop the suffering, and it will end assisted suicide.*[5] The way out of this complex ethical crisis was to promote pain relief and prosecute assisted suicide. Kevorkian was sentenced to prison in Oregon in 1999. In 2000, Congress declared the first decade of the new millennium "The Decade of Pain Control and Research."[6] And so, our attempts to conquer pain and do away with suffering unwittingly opened a Pandora's box. As a country, we started saying *yes* to drugs.

By the time Gen X had babies, extended hospital stays for every procedure were becoming a thing of the past. We had outpatient surgeries and surgery centers, and we were prescribed bottles of the sorts of painkillers previously administered only under the care of watchful hospital staff. Suddenly, everyone in America was granted the permission—and the potent means—to manage our own pain at home. Not just after major surgery or for terminal cancer, but for tooth extractions, backaches, and even headaches.

Pain, the Fifth Vital Sign

It was so easy to get pills in the new millennium. While standard narcotics prescriptions were still carefully regulated and monitored, many of the new opioids and synthetic opioids were not.[7]

On top of that, the American Pain Society pushed to make pain the "fifth vital sign." Unlike the other vital signs checked by medical personnel—blood pressure, heart rate, temperature, and respiratory rate, which have specific and quantifiable standards of measure—pain is subjective.

Brian F. Mandell, MD, PhD, wrote about the staggering effect of the "fifth vital sign movement" in a 2016 issue of the *Cleveland Clinic Journal of Medicine*.[8] Dr. Mandell said that because patients themselves had become the measure, medical personnel were required to accept a patient's word for how much pain they were in. Self-reporting pain became an opportunity for drug manufacturers to market new medications and remarket other drugs *directly to the public* as pain relievers.

Opioids, synthetic opioids, and other non-narcotic drugs flooded the market. Pharmaceutical companies spent billions of dollars each year marketing these new drugs directly to consumers and to physicians through drug reps who assuaged doctors' fears with promises of "non-habit-forming pain relief."[9] Magazine, radio, and television ads for drugs like Tramadol encouraged patients to "ask your doctor if ____ is right for you."

"Step forward in time," Dr. Mandell says, "and pain control has become a measure of patient satisfaction, and thus potentially another physician and institutional rating score that can be linked to reimbursement."[10] In other words, if doctors don't alleviate our pain to our satisfaction, they, their hospital, or their practice could take a financial hit.

Within ten years of pain being established as the fifth vital sign, the number of prescriptions for opioid pain relievers quadrupled to 259 million per year.[11] Medicine cabinets belonging to otherwise clean-living people now contained the potent leftovers of our postsurgical procedures and illnesses—medicines with the addictive properties of heroin—a ready supply for anyone searching for a fix.

We didn't know. No one did. Except the people who got hooked.

In the wake of all those prescriptions, health insurance claims for *opioid dependence* rose **3,000 percent**.[12] By 2011, the problem had become so pervasive that the White House officially recognized prescription drug addiction as an epidemic.

The Centers for Disease Control says 46 people die each day in the United States now from synthetic opioid overdose, more than 200,000 people since 1999. Not from heroin, cocaine, or meth—*from prescription pain relievers*.[13] Paradoxically, back in the 1990s, Jack Kevorkian, whose practice sparked this crusade against pain, assisted in 130 suicides. Total.

Experiments with Pain Treatments

Dave was diagnosed with chronic migraines the year we got married. Pain ruled our early married life. And over time, the migraines became more and more frequent: every holiday, every weekend. We pleaded with God for healing, but the headaches didn't go away. Dave's life outside work became a series of doctor visits and experiments in managing pain.

——⊣ DAVE ⊢——

The first time I went to the doctor for my headaches, they told me I had migraines and gave me a shot of morphine and a bottle of pills to take home. First it was Fiorinal with codeine, and then Vicodin because it was cheaper. Anytime I had a migraine, I'd go back to the doctor and they'd give me more. The pills relieved my pain and let me sleep, but they also gave me a great euphoria and eased the general pains of life as well.

I had migraines so often that if I had a headache at a friend's or relative's house, they'd give me a few of their leftover pain pills, knowing regular pain relievers didn't cut it for me. Over time, I became physically and psychologically dependent on pills to function. But these pills also made me groggy and the frequency of headaches became a concern, not only because I was an otherwise healthy young man in chronic pain, but because I was taking so many narcotics. When I went even a few days without pain pills, I'd begin to experience the flu-like symptoms of withdrawal.

To combat this dependence, my doctors cycled through various narcotics. They experimented with some non-narcotic methods of managing migraines. They tried to get ahead of the pain with beta blockers before it got out of control. They also prescribed a new medication called Imitrex. These self-injections were supposed to open constricted blood vessels thought to be the cause of migraine headaches. They tried IV therapy and even a shot in my eye socket.

At home, we eliminated MSG (monosodium glutamate), which was in nearly all processed foods back then, so Deb made all our meals from scratch. We were careful about strong scents, sleep patterns, and other known migraine triggers.

Because I was so young, I was scanned for brain tumors and tested for allergies, but nothing gave us an explanation for the migraines. And no pain treatments worked very long.

To my relief, and my doctors', four years into my struggle with migraines a new "wonder drug" hit the market. Unlike other prescription pain medications I'd been on, Tramadol was supposedly nonaddictive. This pill promised relief without the typical drowsy side effects of narcotics or danger of dependency.[14]

On Tramadol, I was finally able to be present with my family instead of in bed, in the dark with a pillow over my head. At first, it worked marvelously. So well that I was finally able to manage my life. I was a Christian high school teacher and a basketball and football coach. I worked on the college staff of a large church, teaching and leading small groups. In the summers off from teaching, I worked as a camp director.

Within a year or two, however, I knew I had the same problem I'd had with Vicodin. I had built up a tolerance for Tramadol, which meant I had to take more and more of it to get the same amount of relief I'd had at first. After a while, I started having "rebound headaches" caused by withdrawals between migraine episodes. I started taking Tramadol every day, and several times a day, to keep the withdrawals at bay.

I let myself believe it was okay for me to take so much medication. I felt great on it. It didn't make me sleepy or dopey, and it was easy to get samples and prescriptions.[15] Most drug seekers didn't like it because it didn't give the same euphoria or high that came from drugs like OxyContin and Vicodin. But it worked for me, so, unconcerned that I was becoming a "drug seeker," doctors gave me pill samples for free.

Eventually, though, my need for pills outpaced both my insurance coverage and drug rep samples, and I had to pay out of pocket for multiple prescription refills each month, which was expensive. Although Deb was sympathetic to my pain, the financial strain caused a lot of conflict.

When we were expecting our third baby, I was offered the high school youth pastor job at the church where Deb and I worked as teachers. For a while, I enjoyed the added work, additional pay, and change of ministry. But a year into youth ministry, things started to fall apart again. I was addicted to Tramadol. I just hadn't acknowledged it.

During a particularly bad season for us, I told Deb I thought I'd been running from God and that was why I had so many migraines and money issues. I thought God wanted me to go to seminary to become a pastor and decided on Tacoma, Washington, as a place to start over.

Over the years we've learned that this change-of-scenery and life-overhaul plan is a classic move for someone struggling with addiction. *I just need one magical thing to change outside me and that'll change what's going on inside me*—a new job, a new relationship, a new doctor, a new home—change will fix it without me having to do the work. The problem, of course, is that when

we moved, I went with me. I found new doctors, new pharmacies
. . . and the same struggles.

———— ‖ ————

The Downward Spiral of Addiction

Although most of my (Deb's) family lived near us in California, I
thought the move to Washington would be good for Dave and me.
I hoped he was right and that the stress and strain in our relationship was because he needed to be on another path—like Jonah.
Maybe migraines were Dave's whale, a punishment of sorts for
not doing what he was supposed to be doing, and if he went to
seminary, they'd go away.

Both of us wanted to believe leaving the pace and expense of
life in Southern California would bring much-needed peace to
our home. We weren't just living paycheck to paycheck, we were
living, always, a few months in the hole and the hole was getting
deeper. And so, with the blessing and support of our families and
friends, and four small children—one just weeks old—we moved
a thousand miles so Dave could go to seminary.

In spite of this drastic change, however, Dave's headaches only
increased in frequency, and the tension between us escalated along
with them. I thought I could help him by relieving stress. I kept
parenting and household demands off him as much as I possibly
could, believing it would free him to study and work. A family
member paid Dave's seminary tuition, and I scrimped and saved
to make it possible for me to stay home with our four children
since we had a newborn again. I tried so hard to follow Proverbs
31—the model of wifeliness I was taught in Bible college. I was
going to be a pastor's wife!

But something was wrong. We'd struggled our entire marriage
to keep up with the expense of Dave's chronic pain, but now we
were so poor. Worse off than I'd ever imagined we'd be when we

left our jobs in California—even for a seminary student. After a year and a half of seminary, Dave had passed only one class. And then came a steady stream of collection notices and fear that he was on the verge of losing his job.

I was at a loss to know what to do with our constant conflict. We talked in circles. I tried to reason it out in my head and in my prayers. *How were we here again?* My mind spun with possibilities that pricked my heart with fear. I didn't recognize that Dave was in the downward spiral of addiction.

In the fall of 2003, I turned on the TV for some company while I folded laundry, half listening to *Oprah* until her guest described his wife's mysterious behavior: missing money, failures at work, leaving the house for long periods of time with lame explanations for her absence, elaborate and expensive gifts of reconciliation, effusive apologies—only to go back around through the cycle again.

The story was so familiar to me, I quit folding toddler jeans and matching baby socks and turned up the volume to hear the wife's explanation. The doctors, pharmacies, prescriptions . . . the debts, lies, and excuses—all of it, she said, was to get more drugs.

Oprah turned to the man and asked if he didn't suspect the pills. And he replied that her medications were never a question to him because doctors prescribed them to her for pain. The wife had managed to hide her drug problem from her unsuspecting husband until he accused her of an affair, which was the only reason he could imagine for her deception.

Propelled by curiosity and fear, I dug through our dresser drawers to find discarded Tramadol pill packaging. As many times as I'd picked up prescriptions, I'd never really read all that fine print. It was science, I thought, intended for pharmacists and doctors to decipher. Patients are supposed to just "take as prescribed."

And so, I found myself staring at a large, wispy paper covered with chemistry formulas and symbols, scanning for words that made sense. On the insert for Tramadol, in the fine print, were the words "potential to be highly addictive."

Shocked, I turned to the internet for more. Tramadol *the wonder drug*, the one medication I had never questioned, was a synthetic opioid. On page after page and forum after forum, I found warnings about Tramadol. *Worst withdrawals I've ever had*, I read. *Harder to kick than the heroin.* On and on and on.

I was stunned. Dave having an addiction to his migraine medication was nowhere on my radar. Plus, I didn't believe it was possible for a true Christian, and certainly not one on his way to becoming a pastor, to be addicted to drugs. It seemed impossible for any person who was otherwise living a good, moral life to be a drug addict.

And it wasn't just me! I'd heard it over and over for a decade, sitting beside my husband as we asked doctors questions about the various medications they prescribed. "You don't have an addictive personality," they'd say. "You don't fit the profile." He was a young Christian dad, a youth pastor, a seminary student—not the stereotype of a "drug addict." Not to me, not to medical professionals.

When doctors discovered Tramadol worked for Dave's migraines, he could walk into almost any urgent care clinic with a headache and walk out with a legal prescription. The drug was so new, and so few people asked for it, he often came home with bags full of samples that had just been taking up space on their office shelves.

When a doctor asked with even a hint of skepticism what Dave normally took for pain, he'd visibly relax when he said "Tramadol." You could tell he was relieved Dave hadn't asked for *the hard stuff.*

There were no dealers. No back alleys. Not even a forged prescription. Just a slow, legal descent into addiction—a mirror of the crisis unfolding nationwide.

Admitting Addiction

—┤ DAVE ├—

After that episode of *Oprah*, Deb confronted me. I admitted to her that I was addicted to Tramadol and had probably been struggling with addiction to pills since the first year I was on narcotics—ten years! Drug seeking had overtaken my studies and work. I told her I'd spent a lot of money we didn't have on pills.

But even after confession, I still struggled. I had tried in the past to go a day or two without the pills. I'd attempted to quit pills every morning. I'd wake up saying, "Today, I'm not going to take pills." And then the withdrawals would hit, and I'd be so sick I couldn't handle it.

This time, though, I lost my job, failed seminary classes, and coped with the stress by getting more pills. But Deb knew what to watch for now, and she knew we needed help.

By the time I checked in to rehab, I was taking thirty pills a day. Come to find out, withdrawal from taking high amounts of Tramadol, like I was, is dangerous. They put me in the psychiatric ward of a state hospital, and the physical withdrawal was so severe and violent they had to put me back on Tramadol, wean me off it over a few days, and medicate me through the rest of the detox process.

Once I was stable and drug free, I attended the 12 Step meetings in the rehab unit, and by the end of my three weeks in the hospital, I felt like maybe I was cured. When I got out, I was supposed to go to ninety recovery group meetings in ninety days (the usual instructions when you're released from a 12 Step–based rehab). But I found the meetings intrusive. When you get back to your kids and your life and your church and you have to find a job, and when you don't want other people in your life to know you've been in rehab, it's easy to make excuses not to go to a meeting every night. My hope was to be fixed and changed and not have to deal with it anymore.

I started using pills again within a month. And within three months, I was back to the same level of pills I'd been taking before. I'd take pills, vow to quit, go without them for a few days—sometimes a week—get sick, and go get pills again. Withdrawal triggered migraines, so I was back on the roller coaster. But this time I was more careful to keep not only my purchase but my use of pills hidden from Deb. I lied to her, and I lied to doctors to get pills. I justified the lies to myself, believing I needed them because I couldn't be sick. *I need my job, I need to be present for my family, so I'll just go get a few to get me through this, and then tomorrow I'll taper off them.* Even when I was halfway honest with doctors and told them I'd been in rehab, I'd let them believe it was for OxyContin or Vicodin. They still didn't question Tramadol. (To this day, some rehabs treat opioid addiction with Tramadol.)

———— ‖ ————

I (Deb) wasn't prepared for life after rehab. I didn't understand that escaping addiction involved so much more than just getting off drugs. I didn't realize that even prescription opioids chemically alter a person's brain. I had no idea back then how critical the first ninety days of sobriety are—that *the longer the person in recovery stays clean, the better their chances of staying clean for the long term.*[16] Dave told me he should go to 12 Step meetings. But his commitment to attending them didn't last long, and I didn't fully believe I should encourage attendance. I figured *he had Jesus*, a good pastor to hold him accountable, and for a few months, a weekly meeting with a counselor to help him stay clean. So why should he go get accountability from a group of other addicts? I didn't understand the difference between getting clean and "recovery." And it never crossed my mind that he might relapse.

We told only a handful of people about Dave's addiction problem. As he was still hoping to become a pastor, they advised us to keep it to ourselves. "You won't ever have a ministry if people know," they said, and we knew it was true. Besides, I had hopes he could return to seminary after taking a semester off to work, because I thought he was cured. But Dave didn't go back to seminary. Instead, he got his dream job as the director of a large Pacific Northwest ministry's camp and conference center.

I've since learned that it's hard to detect when dependence on pain pills becomes an addiction. Especially with a drug like Tramadol that didn't make him "high" in a way you could see. Even up to his last days on Tramadol, I couldn't tell the difference between a migraine and withdrawal. But I knew when the bills hit. Or the account was drained. Or I got a collections call. I'd get angry, and he'd be sorry. Over the next three years in ministry, he relapsed into full-blown addiction seven times.

Secrets and Shame

Dave's continued struggle with addiction messed with my theology, my emotions, and my worldview and left me confused, angry, and paralyzed by shame. Both of us had grown up believing abstinence was the surest way to avoid getting ensnared by addiction. We didn't even have alcohol in our home. When in doubt, you simply stayed away from the "gray areas." *Follow the rules, and you'll stay out of trouble. Believe the right things, and you'll stay out of trouble. Right theology*, we'd been taught, *leads to right living.* I never considered taking prescription painkillers for chronic migraines to be a gray area that might "lead to bondage." Yet somehow, we'd gotten into a problem I did not believe good people, let alone Christians, had. Shame convinced me we should keep our problems to ourselves and somehow fix them.

By Dave's fourth relapse, however, I'd had enough of trying to work through our problems alone. We tried pastoral intervention and counseling, and then he had a relapse (#5) . . . Celebrate Recovery (a Christian 12 Step program) . . . and then another relapse (#6). Finally, in desperation, Dave tried an anti-addiction drug called Suboxone (buprenorphine). It worked until keeping the rigorous appointment requirements conflicted too much with his ninety-hour week running summer camp.

That summer, I was full of peace because I thought the combination of 12 Steps and Suboxone were finally working. I didn't know Dave had gone back to buying Tramadol online. With camp money this time, so I wouldn't find out. Relapse number seven.

When Dave finally got clean, it happened in the most painful way I could have imagined. We lost our ministry, our home, and almost our marriage. We crashed so hard, neither of us was sure we could keep going. Our children were devastated and our hearts in ruins. Dave minus pills was a wreck of panic, shame, and acute physical withdrawal. I grasped at the fragments of ravaged faith and begged God to help me find my way through the rubble of our imploded life.

Dave was asked to resign just before the holidays. His wages through the end of the year were garnished entirely to repay a portion of the debt he owed the ministry for buying pills. We found ourselves not only unable to afford a move but entirely unable to care for our family ourselves. We stood helpless at the edge of uncertainty. No jobs, no money, homeless, and deep in debt, and at the lowest our relationship had ever been.

Our needs in those first days, weeks, and months seemed like they would crush us. Although I fully believed God would not let us starve, I felt a nagging disillusionment about exactly what I could expect from a God who, I felt, had let me down so completely. I resisted the way the kids and I had to suffer so much along with Dave. I prayed fervently for a miracle, for a second (third, fourth, fifth) chance for Dave to redeem himself and make everything right. Our kids did too. "Can't you just tell them you're sorry?" they asked.

Beneath the physical needs of our family, my soul was circling the drain. I was shattered by the person I had trusted with my life. He had deceived and betrayed me. Our relationship was in shambles, and for the first time, I didn't care who knew it. All compassion drained from me as I attempted to navigate what felt like the end of hope.

Although I couldn't have told you in those awful days what we needed beyond food and shelter, I'm grateful for a handful of friends who were willing to listen, family who gave us space as best they could while we wrestled with a sort of grief. I even needed the sheriff's deputy who came to our house in response to my 911 hang-up call in the middle of a fight to snap me out of my anger toward my husband before I lost it completely and tore my house down with my own hands.[17]

Dave, who was even further down the drain than me, needed to know there was hope for *him*, and I was in no place myself to encourage him. He had finally emptied my reservoir of compassion, and others had to step in for a while and let me refill.

What we did not anticipate from the bottom of our pit was the generosity of the community around us—compassion offered by some of the same people we'd tried so hard to hide our brokenness from for three years. Former employees, still sorting through their own response to Dave's fall from leadership, gave us money for food and our move off the camp property. A family from our church let us stay in their home for a while. Dave's parents squeezed us all into their two-bedroom condominium for a couple of months. Our pastor and our new recovery community continued to offer encouragement and friendship.

This outpouring of kindness gave me the taste of God's compassion I needed in order to get out of bed in the morning and face the sadness of my children, the moodiness of my disconsolate husband, and the task of packing up our house in sorrow. I couldn't see beyond the next meal, let alone make decisions for our future. The compassion of individuals in our community propped me up, gave me hope, and kept me alive. And it overwhelmed Dave, who was sure everyone hated him.

Unbind Lazarus

By chapter 11 of John's Gospel, Jesus is three years into his public ministry, and he has established a reputation for healing. So when Lazarus gets sick, and his sisters send for Jesus, they have faith he will heal their brother just like he's healed so many others. Instead, Jesus sends word back to Mary and Martha: "This sickness will not end in death. No, it is for God's glory so that God's Son may be glorified through it."[18] And so, the sisters hold on to the hope of healing, even as they watch their brother's condition get worse.

John reports that Jesus stays away from the town of Bethany two agonizing days longer. To be fair, the leaders in Bethany had just tried to stone him . . . but whatever the reason for delay, without Jesus there to heal him, Lazarus gets sicker. And then he dies. When Jesus finally returns to Bethany, the sisters greet him, weeping, and his heart breaks with love and compassion. Jesus, who could have prevented this death, weeps beside the mourners!

A crowd of family, friends, skeptics, and spies gathers around Jesus and the sisters and follows the mourners to the tomb. When the village is assembled, Jesus says to them, "Take away the stone." Martha objects. *Lazarus has been dead for days and it will stink!* They all know it's true. The smell will be horrible. But they do it anyway, *because it's Jesus*, and everyone—no matter what their motive at this point—is hoping for a miracle.

So Jesus prays loudly. And then he shouts so everyone around can hear: "Lazarus! Come out!" And miraculously, Lazarus, who was absolutely, unquestionably dead a minute ago, emerges from the tomb with his hands and feet and face still wrapped like a mummy. His appearance must have caused quite a stir. I'm sure the crowd stared in awe, perhaps anticipating a magical transformation of mummy into man. Instead, Jesus turns to the mesmerized crowd and tells *them* to finish the job: "Unbind him, and let him go."[19]

With that command, suddenly setting Lazarus free from the shroud of death and restoring him to life becomes a community effort.

Charles Haddon Spurgeon preached in the 1880s about this unexpected plot twist: "This seems a strange sequel to a miracle. The bands of death released, but not the bands of linen; motion given, but not movement of hand or foot, strength bestowed, but not the power to undress himself."[20] So the community of bystanders followed Jesus's command and unwrapped Lazarus's hands, his feet, his face. And their care for him likely didn't end there. Spies had witnessed this resurrection and reported it back to religious leaders who now wanted to kill not only Jesus but Lazarus as well, because he was living proof of Jesus's claim to be God.

Jesus had said this pivotal moment would show God's glory. With this command, Jesus is allowing the willing bystanders to touch a piece of that glory. Wrapped up in this miracle was the transfer of the ministry of restoration from Jesus to the community. So Spurgeon turns the story back around to us: "This brings us to consider a timely assistance which you and I are called to render. Oh, for wisdom to learn our duty, and grace to do it at once."[21]

Breaking free from addiction, no matter how it comes about, is a sort of miracle. But sobriety is just the beginning. Recovery is a process, not a onetime event. At the heart of recovery is the compassion of a community of bystanders willing to help complete the work of restoration.

Every single person who touched our lives in that year left a significant mark on our family. Without knowing it, each one became a strand of a tightly woven safety net that caught all six of us, not just Dave, when he fell. Our family, some dear friends, our recovery group, our church, our kids' public school, doctors, employers, counselors, teachers, even a community theater—helped restore not only Dave but all of us to life. It took a village. A community. Just as it did for Lazarus.

. . . .

Addiction thrives in secret. It wraps tight around, binding hands and feet in strips of shame. Suffocating, blinding, burying. Refusing to release. We cannot wrench anyone from the tomb-grip of addiction, and we are powerless to raise them from living death.

There is nothing we can do to force life into them. We can only give God our grief, stand by, and pray for a miracle.

I wanted to believe the miracle of healing I'd prayed for had happened that day when Dave was forced out of the grave, that God's glory would come out of our pain and grief in spite of the devastating aftermath. In that hour, as one person and then another stepped toward us, healing began.

If you haven't already experienced the challenges of being part of someone's safety net, chances are, you will. And when you have the blessing of standing nearby when someone finally breaks free from the death grip of an addiction, you have an opportunity to be a part of restoring them fully to life. You simply have to be a willing bystander.

two

Reviving Compassion

> No one person can fulfill all your needs. But the community can truly hold you. The community can let you experience the fact that, beyond your anguish, there are human hands that hold you and show you God's faithful love.
>
> HENRI NOUWEN

> When they cried out to you again, you heard from heaven, and in your compassion you delivered them time after time.
>
> NEHEMIAH 9:28

Addiction leaves a wide path of destruction in its wake. In the body, in a family, in the community around the person in addiction. The addict himself or herself may have numbed themselves so much that when they emerge from the death grip of addiction, they're overwhelmed by the damage they've done in their life. Relationships need to be mended, debts paid, jobs found. Living drug free and starting over is packed with obstacles and doubts:

*My family won't forgive me, my friends won't have anything
to do with me, my wife left, no one will hire me. . . .* Setting
everything right again seems impossible. The only way for them
to move forward without becoming immobilized by overwhelming discouragement is to take one step at a time in the right
direction.

But for those of us who've been waiting, praying, begging God
for healing, we're ready for them to be healthy *right now.* "One
step at a time" feels too slow!

The healing process can't move fast enough for us. Either we're
ready to pick up, move on, and forget the past; or we want our
loved one to start in right away on making up for everything they
did wrong in their addiction. We want them to be sorry. We want
them to recognize the damage they caused. We want to see reform!
*The last thing we want to hear is that our patience is needed now
as much as it ever was.*

It's difficult to accept that getting clean is just the beginning
of our prayers being answered. Recovery is a whole-life healing
process. When a person makes the decision to get sober, it's just
the start of their recovery journey. They're setting out on a path
to clean up not only themselves but every aspect of their life.

In her memoir, *The Big Fix: Hope after Heroin,* Tracey Helton Mitchell says, "The real work comes after you put down the
drugs."[1] While drug addicts have a 40 to 60 percent chance of
relapse in the first ninety days, studies show 85 percent of individuals relapse and return to drug use within one year of treatment.[2]
Getting clean is a huge step, but it's only half the story.

The Side Effects of Addiction

Addiction brings all kinds of garbage with it. If someone close to
you has been living in addiction, you know this. You've been living with the side effects too. Physical, mental, relational, spiritual,
financial, legal—they carry grief and shame, both for the drug

abuser and for you. *These side effects don't resolve the minute an addict breaks free from drugs.*

And though a hidden addiction like prescription drugs or alcoholism may result in different consequences from addiction to illegal drugs, to some degree, they all share the same side effects. Even when active addiction seems to have stopped, financial insecurity, relational conflicts, depression, health problems, and employment issues can linger for years. We have to remember that our relationship to the person in recovery is just one of many areas where change is needed.

Physical Side Effects

—H DAVE—

Drug abuse does a good deal of damage to the body and brain. Getting fully clean from some drugs—including prescriptions— can take months. The first days and weeks of detoxing from drugs can be dangerous and even deadly. Because of the length of time and the amount of Tramadol I was taking, my detox in 2004, the spring of 2007, and again in December of 2007 were all medically supervised through this acute withdrawal stage. Physical healing was slow. I was jittery and irritable, I felt like I had the flu, and I had difficulty focusing for more than a few minutes for several weeks.

After detox, I suffered from post-acute withdrawal syndrome (PAWS), which was less physical but more mental, for months. I finally started feeling more normal about six months after my last tapered dose of a short course of buprenorphine (a detox medication discussed more in chap. 11).

Some damage from drug abuse stays with you. I still have some trouble with concentration and focus—eleven years later. And because of the amount of drugs I'd taken, doctors were concerned about my liver and kidneys for almost ten years after my last pill.

We don't all respond to drugs the same way. There's always someone who successfully "went cold turkey" to get free from drugs. But the potential for complications or even death makes it risky. In addition to severe physical withdrawal, shame, fear, money and insurance issues can keep addicts from reaching for and receiving the help they need to recover.

———⅋———

Relational Side Effects

Drug addicts have a lot of faults. Although many problems like forgetfulness, irritability, and inattentiveness can be attributed to the effects of substance abuse on their brains, we can't deny that the choices they've made and compulsions they've exhibited have hurt people around them. Distancing and damaging behaviors like abuse, lying, stealing from friends and family, neglect, belligerence, and defensiveness are hard to get past and make it difficult to mend relationships. It's natural and human to be skeptical and self-protective even when a person in recovery from addiction seems genuinely penitent.

A friend of ours who hires men in recovery to work in his business says *it's easier to love someone when their past behavior hasn't hurt you personally.* It's true. As compassionate as we may feel toward strangers, most of us can't just easily erase offenses and start from zero when it's been so personal and damaging. Although we may wish we could just sweep the past under the rug as though it never happened, in the closest relationships, like marriage, lingering damage has to be addressed for real healing to take place.

The process of healing a marriage devastated by addiction can be long and difficult and may require the professional help of a counselor—not only for the spouse but for the addict. Often, addiction has been a coping mechanism covering feelings of shame or inadequacy or fear, and finally addressing those hidden, toxic wounds can bring whole-life healing. In cases where abuse and/or unfaithfulness were side effects of addiction, mending a marriage may take a miracle or a lot of work or both, but we've seen it happen.

Spiritual and Psychological Side Effects

Newly sober people deal with spiritual side effects as well. In recovery, over time, former addicts begin to take stock of where they've been, seek forgiveness from people they've hurt, and learn to accept themselves as a beloved child of God. They may have experienced rejection by the church and by spiritual mentors. They may have had public disgrace. Their deep shame or trouble in managing co-occurring issues (like veterans in recovery also dealing with post-traumatic stress) may be a massive barrier to stepping foot inside a church, or even coming home again.

They may struggle with anxiety, depression, and regret for a long time, especially if their addiction led to losses like divorce or jail or losing custody of their children. No matter how many times we repeat a message of forgiveness, that sort of pain doesn't disappear and may never fully heal in this life. Even in recovery, many former addicts are living every day with the tragic and painful consequences of their addiction.

Financial Side Effects

The financial toll of addiction is obvious when an addict ends up couch surfing or sleeping on the streets. But the cost to families who have successfully hidden their "problem" from the public can be devastating. Private detox, rehab, and long-term recovery programs cost thousands and even tens of thousands of dollars. "Multiple trips through detox, rehab, and sober houses can take a financial toll that's almost beyond belief," writes Anne M. Fletcher in *Inside Rehab*.[3]

Addicts, even functioning ones whose addiction hides beneath a thin veil of competence, drive themselves and their families deep into debt and lose jobs, homes, cars, as they continue to buy expensive drugs. Addiction propels people toward payday loans, high-interest credit cards, and other predatory lending traps.

Though some employers are now working to implement intervention programs for recovery, coming clean about prescription drug addiction costs many people their jobs: nurses, pastors, police officers, social workers, and more. As ready as a person in recovery may be to be responsible and work hard as a newly restored person, finding or keeping meaningful work that provides for their family will be very hard. Being fired, felony possession, serving time in prison, gaps in employment for rehab, and even poor credit ratings are major barriers for future employment and housing.

Understanding Recovery

—⊣ DAVE —

In its simplest terms, **recovery is a return to health.** We understand this with wounds we can see. If you break your leg badly enough, you'll have a long return to full health, involving surgery, traction, and rehabilitation through physical therapy. Your recovery process will depend on the severity of the trauma, your age, and your diligence with the exercises you're prescribed. And what happens if you never fully recover your former strength? You might always walk with a limp, and your habits will change. Maybe you'll stop climbing mountains because walking on an incline for more than a mile knocks you out for weeks. In the same way, recovery is more than just living without the object of your addiction. It's learning a new way of life.

Recovery takes time. People don't get into addiction overnight. It can happen through a series of poor choices, or it can happen through a series of legal prescriptions, or both. It took time to dig the hole and it will take time to get out. The damage you've done in your addiction doesn't go away when you stop using. It takes time to mend relationships, rebuild homes and careers. It takes time to form new habits and to put into practice new ways of coping with stress or grief. It takes time to recognize and process underlying issues. It takes time to regain trust—and to trust. And it takes time to get back on your feet financially. Recovery is learning how to live without the drug or drink that has helped you get by for so long *at the same time* as you are trying to build a healthier life.

———— ⊞ ————

Recovery is individual and can't be mapped out perfectly. It may worry us when our loved one's recovery doesn't take the path, or go at the speed, *we* think it should. It's amazing how quickly we ourselves can relapse into the old ways of relating to our loved one when they relapse. If we believe in oppression or possession, demons will be cast out. If we believe good, consistent discipline will correct as bad a "habit" as addiction, we'll go after heavy-duty accountability and reform. If we believe it's a disease, we'll seek medical solutions, maybe even pills to remedy pill addiction. If we believe it's a disorder, we'll pursue psychological solutions. In our house, we tried them all.

We all want one universal answer—one "magic pill" to fix our problem. But addiction involves body, soul, and mind. You can't make a perfect script for recovery. None of us are wired exactly the same, so it's vital to remember that what works for one person may not work for another. Everyone heals at their own pace. You can't force it or make it go faster. Sometimes people seem healed and then they relapse. This is soul-crushing for loved ones and can leave us feeling helpless and defeated. To avoid this, we are tempted to try to manage their recovery just as we tried to manage them out of their addiction.

Releasing Control over Recovery

The hardest thing for us to do at this point in the journey is to recognize our place in our loved one's recovery story. We are the bystanders, not the healer, at Lazarus's tomb. We can help a loved one as they wrestle free from the bondage of addiction and from the side effects that threaten to pull them back into their grave.

What does "unbinding Lazarus" look like in recovery terms? It means we live in a tension between wanting to do what's best and not knowing what that is. We waver between kindness and anger and walk a tightrope, trying so hard to do everything exactly right—fearful of making a mistake.

We don't want to be *codependent* or to *enable* because we've heard those things are bad. So we read books, go to seminars, support groups, and counselors—all good things. But if we're honest with ourselves, there are times we say we're seeking discernment when what we're really after is to be told how to fix it all. We want a predetermined plan of action—a flowchart of if/then scenarios. And then, we stick obstinately with our plan because, whether we acknowledge it or not, applying "tough love" tactics can numb us to the heartache of being disappointed yet again.

Understanding Real Codependency

For the past few decades, anyone in a relationship with a person struggling with addiction has automatically been labeled "codependent." Melody Beattie, whose book *Codependent No More* is considered a foundational recovery textbook, broadened the scope of codependent to "one who has let another person's behavior affect him or her, and who is obsessed with controlling that person's behavior."[4] There are many helpful and important principles in Beattie's books and the dozens of other books about codependency—especially for those in recovery from addiction or who suffer severe anxiety over pleasing others.

But if we are going to love sacrificially like Jesus, we have to be careful how strictly and specifically we apply them or any guides. We have to use discernment. Breaking free from codependent habits can become legalistic—the same as can happen with so many good principles for living. Beverly Engel, therapist and bestselling author of an abundance of recovery resources, sums up the problem with applying codependency principles too broadly:

> Loved ones have often been told that the best way to help their substance dependent partner or family member is *not* to help. Those with codependent behavior have often been told to "detach with love" or to practice "tough love." Partners and family members worry about doing anything nice for their loved one for fear of "enabling" their destructive behavior. But contrary to these admonishments research has shown that partners of those who are substance dependent can actually play an important role in helping their partner to change.⁵

In other words, even when our hearts have said *love, forgive, welcome home*, out of fear of hindering recovery by our kindness we lean into the "experts" who have laid out plans for tough love, strict boundaries, and detachment. "Detachment" in the context of codependency means *everyone is responsible for their own behavior*. But detachment can quickly turn cold, harsh, and even manipulative if we aren't careful. If we are being honest, we often draw our boundaries and detach to protect ourselves from disappointment or to force change. Forced change might be effective in some circumstances, but not all. When a person's recovery is fragile and they are struggling, "zero tolerance" may only feed their debilitating shame and lead to hiding out of fear, or to relapse, or to giving up completely.

The result is that we stifle our urge to fling our arms open wide like the father in Jesus's parable and welcome home a prodigal who doesn't have it all together yet. Not to say letting someone suffer the consequences of their choices isn't necessary, but our responses must take underlying issues and any forward progress into consideration. Accepting that we can't control our loved one's recovery doesn't mean we should cut them out of our lives until they achieve the level of faithfulness and responsibility we wish they had. Cutting them out of our life completely can be just another form of control on our part.

Drawing a distinction between acting from love and acting from self-protection and fear, Dale and Juanita Ryan, founders of the National Association for Christian Recovery, offer these insights into true codependency:

- "Codependent behaviors are panic reactions to another person's addiction or compulsion."
- "Codependency is rooted in a drive to do it all, and do it perfectly."
- Codependents derive their value from what they do and work themselves into over-responsibility for everyone and everything.
- Codependency is rooted in denial of problems and painful emotions.
- And codependents believe "that happiness in life is a direct result of another person's behavior."[6]

Recovery professionals like Beattie, Engel, and the Ryans don't limit codependency to nonaddicts; rather, they know it's one of the root causes of addiction itself. And codependency doesn't have to be related to addiction at all.

So how do we know where the line is? "When we are being truly compassionate," says Engel, "our intentions are motivated by love and selflessness. In contrast, the underlying motive of co-dependency is self-protection."[7]

Maybe our problem is that we've been trying so hard to respond "correctly" rather than compassionately.

Embracing Empathy and Connection

Jack Deere describes how he wrestled with conventional wisdom in his memoir *Even in Our Darkness*. His wife, Leesa, battled addiction to the alcohol and drugs she used to drown out child-hood trauma and her grief over their son's suicide. Deere consulted counselors who advised boundaries, detachment, and even divorce if Leesa didn't stop drinking.

Deere and his wife separated for a time, and he writes of that season: "I met with a counselor each week. We talked about boundaries, healthy limits on the type of interactions we will allow. Boundaries protect us, keep us from being used, and bring a sense of order to our lives. But like any good thing, they can be misused. . . . I had told her that she had to be fixed before I would take her back. If God had treated me like that, I could never draw near to him."[8] We are, all of us, flawed human beings.

Experts now say the chances of a person in recovery from ad-diction staying clean increase when they have *encouragement* from their community, rather than being cut off. One study sums it up this way: "Social support from family and friends has been consis-tently found to predict positive outcomes" in addiction recovery.[9] This isn't just support when they're following our guidelines and boundaries. This is unconditional love.

In his popular TED talk "Everything You Think You Know about Addiction Is Wrong" (viewed more than nine million times as of this writing), *Chasing the Scream* author Johann Hari ends with the bold claim that "the opposite of addiction is connec-tion."[10] While connection may not be the exact antithesis of addic-tion, Hari's statement that connection and community are related to sustained long-term addiction recovery is not really a new idea, but it feels somewhat revolutionary after decades of tough love, boundaries, and detachment.

If you look closely, you'll see there is a revival of compassion taking place in our culture. Who would have thought a comedian like Russell Brand would become a pseudo-evangelist for recov-ery, calling addicts out of the darkness of their secret shame and provoking us to move toward grace? Russell Brand and research storytellers like Brené Brown and Johann Hari use words like *empathy* and *connection* to describe compassionate behaviors, but the "new" ideas they're talking about have been foundational Christian truths for centuries, expressed in the Bible as *mercy*, *grace*, and *compassion*.

Empathy is "understanding another person's thoughts, feelings, and condition from his or her point of view, rather than from one's own."[11] Jesus modeled empathy when he cried at Lazarus's tomb. Though he knew the outcome would be joyful, he wept because he connected with Mary and Martha's grief. Empathy was part of his mission on earth: "For we do not have a high priest who is unable to empathize with our weaknesses."[12] As Christians, we're called to suffer together, and bear one another's burdens. We're called to restore broken people to community—to connection. Paul writes about this in 2 Corinthians 2:7, following his admonition to bring someone who has been punished: "Forgive and comfort him, so that he will not be overwhelmed by excessive sorrow." God calls us to weep with those who weep.

Connection and empathy are vital to reconciliation. We've just been sidetracked by theological, political, psychological, medical, and relational debates that have become roadblocks to the simple truth. In our *all or nothing, either/or* society, we've lost sight of the individual, the person struggling with addiction. Compassion is not a formula. Compassion isn't bad. It's biblical, emanating from genuine care and concern.

When we take a closer look at what's underneath addiction, we might find a co-occurring disorder, abuse, trauma, mental illness. Are they high-functioning? Maybe they are crippled by a need to please and succeed and their drug of choice gives them courage. And this becomes an underlying reason for their addiction. The draw of prescription drugs for white-collar workers is similar to alcoholism. *I need this fix to do my job, manage my home, take care of Mom well.*

When we apply our "tough love" practices of shape up or ship out, it merely confirms the fear that they are not enough on their own without drugs. In order to heal, it's so important to get at the root of their addiction. But allowing people to be less than perfect is tough in our performance-based American culture. Somewhere along the way, we've dismissed these biblical principles as ineffective in circumstances like addiction. Have we stopped encouraging love that *endures*, *hopes*, *and believes* because we think common sense should overrule? All of us need grace, but we hesitate to give it out. "We accept grace in theory but deny it in practice,"[13] wrote Brennan Manning.

Rather than resulting in effective change for addicts in recovery, our application of tough love has evolved into intolerance for woundedness, weakness, and humanness. If we believe God restores people and relationships, we need always to come back to the hardest truths about love. Life-changing love can be messy. Love binds us together, and it also costs us something.

Reviving Compassion: the Antidote to Shame

"Compassion is the most powerful tool you can have when it comes to healing addiction of any kind,"[14] Christopher Kennedy Lawford and Beverly Engel write in their 2016 book, *When Your Partner Has an Addiction*. And add that "compassion is especially effective when it comes to healing shame, which as we've seen is closely connected to addiction. . . . Compassion is, as it turns out, the only antidote to shame—the only thing that can counteract and neutralize shame's isolating, stigmatizing, debilitating poison."[15]

Isn't this how God treats us? "The LORD is gracious and compassionate, slow to anger and rich in love."[16] His love and compassion grant us mercy, and our response to his mercy is change.

—H DAVE—

After clearing the decks of all pretense in Romans 1, the apostle Paul says none of us have a leg to stand on as far as judging one another goes. "Do you show contempt for the riches of his kindness, forbearance and patience, not realizing that God's kindness is intended to lead you to repentance?"[17]

We're called to be the expression of God's compassion to each other, not the expression of his judgment. Compassion isn't just an abstract idea. It's not saying, *I'll love you when you're good enough* or *I'll love you when you've gotten your act together*. Grace and compassion are specifically extended when we don't deserve it. Mercy is compassion in action. It's God's kindness *plus* his help. It's forbearance. It's long-suffering, and it involves time and patience and hope.

But if your community is more concerned with appearance and managing behavior, you learn that the only way to receive love and kindness is by performance. We have to recognize and let go of our own "addictions": the need to be right, the need to be comfortable, the need for a plan or checklist, the need for payback. If your community is willing to show you what grace looks like by giving you a third, fourth, eighth chance, then you begin to understand grace. That doesn't mean we always let things go or that there are never any consequences, but there are times when walking through consequences *with* the one who has been in the wrong is an expression of Christlike compassion.

"But I'm not God." We hear this a lot. We depend on God's grace and forgiveness for us, but when we look at an addict whose life is in shambles, our stuff doesn't look so bad. We forget we're all in need of mercy. So when we withhold compassion, in effect we're saying, *I'm worthy of grace and you're not. Because I gave you grace and you violated it. I'll give you grace as long as I can verify you're worthy of it.* It requires faith to look at someone who's hurt us, who says they're trying to make it right, and give them the benefit of the doubt.

The burden of loving a person in recovery from addiction is heavy. But we don't have to practice compassion alone. Compassion and community go together. God can miraculously help us as individuals, but he's put the church here for a reason. We are to be known by our love for each other.

Practicing Compassion in Community

Disconnecting from an addict until they prove to you they're never going to fail again doesn't achieve the desired turnaround. It didn't work for me—the addict mind always thinks, "I can get around the negative consequence." Being the object of wrath helped me live with the disconnect. But it's a different thing for an addict to worry about throwing away love, compassion, and forgiveness.

Adherence to strict boundaries and laws didn't make God's people righteous. Jesus instituted a new covenant when he became our means to restoration with God. In the Old Testament, God says, *Obey and I will bless you.* In the New Testament, God says, *I love you, period.* And then we love him, because he loves us.[18] We don't understand God's limitless love for us. That's why the parables are so practical. The prodigal son, the good Samaritan. They show us how to love our neighbor as ourselves. We're defeated by ultimatums and impossible standards, but a call to holiness coupled with compassion and patience compels us to accept God's forgiveness and love and strive to become more like him.

In my addiction, and for many years of my recovery, I struggled to forgive myself and accept God's grace. I felt that for Deb and others to forgive me, I needed to be worthy of forgiving. It was a terrifying thought that I could try to do my best and still end up not being forgiven. The most powerful and motivating thing for me is that people saw my grossest self and loved me anyway. Love was more motivating than pain.

Changing your life forever takes time. Patience is critical in the change process. Without it, you'll give up hope. There's a lot of trying and failing in the recovery process, but failure doesn't necessarily mean the process isn't moving forward. That's not to say relapse shouldn't be taken seriously—it should. The longer you go without a relapse, the better your chances of recovery. But the motivation to try again after failure comes from the hope that recovery is actually possible.

When we ask for too much from a person in recovery all at once, we set them up for failure. The recovery process is unique to each person, and their journeys may all follow a similar pattern but each in their own time. We can't rush it. Rushing recovery is what got us into this opioid crisis in the first place. Getting clean and staying clean is a consuming process—some of the things we want addicts to do force them to sacrifice things they know they need to do for their recovery. The good news is, no matter who we are in an addicted person's life, we don't have to do this compassion thing alone. The call to compassion does come with a partner to strengthen and multiply its power: community. But for the grace of God and the unwitting safety net that caught us, I know we wouldn't have made it through. And certainly not together.

To some extent, every person in an addict's close community has to face their beliefs, ideas, biases, and engage the person in front of them as an individual, not a disease or sin or whatever label we have put on them. Chances are, we aren't dealing with a mass of addicts, probably just one or maybe two. We can address them as people, not as their addiction.

Committing to the Process

Recovery requires a new commitment on all sides. On one side, it's an acknowledgment by the addict that *my addictive behavior has been destructive, not only to me, but also to the people in my life, and I am ready to do what it takes to change and live as a healthy, contributing member of my family and society.* On the other side, we—their friend, spouse, church—have to make a choice. Are we going to go on this journey with them?

Dave's journey challenged everything I thought I already knew about love, forgiveness, and grace. When I first realized his dependence on pain pills had become an addiction, I treated it solely as a struggle with sin. To heal from addiction, I believed Dave would need to confess and repent, and then he'd be healed. With some accountability, and maybe a little counseling, he'd stay clean because his heart was clean. I didn't call it "recovery"; I called it "walking with the Lord." The only language I had to describe relapse was that he was "backsliding" or "wrestling with besetting sin." I believed good, consistent discipline would correct his drug habit. I got pretty good at confrontation and interrogation. And most of those sessions would end with Dave being very sorry and making a commitment to change.

Then his relapses would throw me into a tailspin. I couldn't fathom how a person who was so contrite could return to his sins. We investigated every possibility we could think of: addiction was a disease, addiction was demonic oppression, addiction was a disorder. We did none of this seeking openly, because in Christian culture and in the whole of society, his addiction was wrong and we were ashamed of it.

My mistake, however, and Dave's too, was in thinking if he could just get the drugs out of his system, he would return to his former self and start making good choices with his life. We'd go through months without evidence of his addiction, and suddenly there it was: a bill, a collections call, and the sound of a bottle of pills being opened in the night.

Our marriage, my love, and my faith were strained through the fine mesh of 1 Corinthians 13: *love is patient, love is kind. . . .* I didn't know what to do with my anger. At times, I wielded it as a protective shield, covering my hurt and fear. If I could just convince Dave that he was not loving me, not loving the kids, not loving God, not being a good person because of his addiction, he would change. But no threat, no plea, no prayer seemed to break through and change him.

The tools we use to try to change our loved one depend on our personality, our understanding of addiction, our faith. But at some point, we come to realize our methods are useless. Maybe, like me, you saw that when you finally let go of fixing the addiction, you actually gave God room to work in your husband, your wife, your child, or your friend. The temptation we all face in this new place called "recovery" is to go back to our old ways of dealing with our loved one, including our fears, our anger, and our sadness. Our response to their addiction often becomes our response during their recovery.

It's so easy to revert to being demanding and exacting, and to hold firm to harsh boundaries and unrealistic expectations. Sure, our threats or emotional interventions may have gotten them into rehab, but that mode of relating to our loved one will not sustain their recovery. In the 12 Step process, a humble heart is the first step to recovery. Admitting "I can't do this on my own" opens the door to help, health, and freedom. When your loved one is willing to seek help, it's not the time for rejection or ultimatums.

Yes, this is scary. When we let go of managing our loved one's recovery from addiction, we are letting go of control of something that may have a huge effect on us—anything can happen. Letting go, for me, meant I could be surprised again. And not good surprise. Awful surprise.

three

A Marriage in Recovery

> I wish we could sometimes love the characters in real life as we love the characters in romances. There are a great many human souls whom we should accept more kindly, and even appreciate more clearly, if we simply thought of them as people in a story.
>
> G. K. CHESTERTON

> Love never gives up, never loses faith, is always hopeful, and endures through every circumstance.
>
> 1 CORINTHIANS 13:7 NLT

From May 2013 to November 2014, the *Guardian UK* website ran an anonymous weekly column titled "A Marriage in Recovery." In the series, the author documents her husband's addiction and her reactions. She drives herself mad pushing him to get clean. He's sober for a few months, and then he relapses.[1]

"My feelings were a confused mixture of anger, worry, and uselessness," the author says. "I set ultimatums I later broke. All my conflicting demands in our relationship of 'Get out!' then 'Why aren't you at home?' then 'Tell me the truth for God's sake!' (my behaviour was as mixed up as his) created a toxic environment for a family."[2]

She learns about codependency and struggles to save her sanity by following conventional wisdom to "detach" from him. When she finally relinquishes responsibility for him to change, he does. And then he relapses again.

The author's husband ends up in rehab and comes home with the usual post-rehab prescription to attend ninety 12 Step meetings in ninety days. However, the commitment to his recovery program causes friction in their relationship. Everything in their life now revolves around his recovery, while the writer feels she is still bearing the weight of family responsibility alone and shouldn't have to. She writes bitterly, "Most evenings my husband is staying late at work, going to AA meetings or letting off steam on the running machine. *I want a life.*"[3]

Because she's so stressed taking care of the kids alone, her husband eventually stops going to AA meetings to help out at home. He turns to his own stress-coping mechanisms, and ultimately, he relapses again. The author kicks him out for a while. And later, when he moves back in, sober again, the peace in their home scares her, because she doesn't trust him fully. She's always tense, waiting for the other shoe to fall. "One of the hardest things about living with addiction," she writes, "is the not-knowing."[4]

This is what it's really like to let go. Acknowledging we can't control our spouse's recovery any more than we could control their addiction is one thing, but really acting on that understanding is infinitely more difficult. Supporting their recovery requires sacrifice. Plus, we are only human, and our fears are real.

The Ashes of Addiction

The thing that broke *our* marriage wasn't the addiction itself, strange as it seems. It was all the side effects: instability, loneliness, poverty, fear, and above all, the lies. The damage done by deception is soul-shattering. Betrayal of trust is hard to overcome. Impossible in a marriage, really, without grace.

High-functioning addicts, whose addiction is masked by the appearance of normalcy, become masters of deception. They become particularly good at it when they're addicted to prescription drugs because they've had to learn how to deceive medical personnel in order to legally obtain their drug of choice. When you lie that well, that often, you begin to believe your own lies so much that you hardly realize you are lying.

Deception gradually creeps into a marriage eroding from addiction and may build over a long period of time. When the pain prescription after your own surgery ran out so quickly, you questioned your spouse about the missing pills and his answer was, "You must have miscounted." When your power was turned off because of unpaid electric bills, it was, "I told you I paid it, there must be some mistake." When he started seeing different doctors: "Dr. Jones couldn't fit me in, so I went to the urgent care." These are not outlandish lies. They are subtle, entirely believable, deceptions.

And maybe, in the back of your mind, you are always questioning. When the balloon you were inflating with suspicion burst and you finally asked outright, "Are you using?" he swore he wasn't. And yet it happened again, and again, and again. Not only has he lied to you, but the reality is he's probably stolen prescription medication from you, your kids, your family, your friends. There's a ripple effect that goes beyond the two of you. If you've been married to someone who struggles with an addiction, you know this dance too well. The conflict between desperately wanting the truth and wishing you could live in denial makes you feel crazy. Eventually, because you'd rather not trust yourself than not trust the person you love, you learn to question your *own* mind and perceptions.

This is not a "fix it with a weekend marriage getaway" situation.

The Reality of Restoration

Our marriage wasn't just a fixer-upper; it was a "value is in the land" sort of listing. Honestly, *just rip it all down to the foundation and start over.* After so many years, our patterns of relating to each other were off-the-charts bad. Moving forward for us meant learning a new relationship with each other while simultaneously dealing with collateral damage. When so much devastation has been done in a marriage, the road beyond forgiveness to reconciliation has few travelers.

Why is this true when culturally we're enamored with the idea of loving a person to wholeness? If you're familiar with the bestselling Christian novel *Redeeming Love* (the book of Hosea, fictionalized and set in the American West), you know the story makes a tantalizing romance novel. But in real life, restoring a marriage broken by betrayal and deception goes beyond romance to ridiculous. It's a foolish fantasy. This is because most of us—no matter what we believe about love, life, and faith—have limits. Whether we call them "boundaries" or not, we'll only "put up with" so much.

Rebuilding a marriage eroded by deception takes a kind of commitment that building it did not require. When you first get married, you face challenges all starry-eyed and positive. But on the other side of addiction, there's not a whole lot of excitement in the challenges ahead. Maybe for years you've been holding your family together and just can't take any more uncertainty. Or maybe you've been here before, but a relapse devastated you and now you're skeptical—with good reason.

Betrayal of trust is no small thing, and restoring trust is everything for healing a broken marriage.

Staying through the mess of recovery in the wake of addiction is not popular, even among Christians. And it's countercultural these days to live out the belief that people can change. This makes staying together and working through the hardest places in marriage a lonely venture.

In Recovery, Not Recovered

The in-between space called "recovery" is complicated for a marriage. There's a measure of uncertainty, especially if you've been through it before and your spouse has relapsed. And if there's been separation of any sort—even so your spouse could go through a long-term recovery program—the adjustment to being together again will very likely be tempestuous. Expectations collide. Your spouse in recovery may not be doing drugs or abusing alcohol anymore, but there's no way for you as their partner to really know how healed they are. Though you wish for proof, there's nothing that will fully assure you of their healing except when they've proven themselves over time. And allowing for the proof of time means that for a while your relationship may be just as hard as it ever was during full-blown addiction.

Maybe while your spouse was away in rehab you got into your own rhythm with the kids. It's hard for your spouse to find their place in the family again. Or maybe, as in the story from the *Guardian*, and in many other families we've known, you are exhausted from playing the single parent for all the time they were in addiction and then rehab, and now you are not only ready for a break—you deserve one! You can hardly wait for your spouse to pick up the slack.

Emotions run high all around, and so does fear of failure. You're having to practice a delicate balance of trust and wisdom. What is reasonable to expect from your spouse, and what is reasonably required of you? How do you both adjust your expectations? *And what if you're not ready for them to be home?*

As much as it was a financial strain for Dave to be in rehab the first time, and as hard as it was to parent four little kids alone, my consolation was *at least he was in a place where he couldn't do more damage to us or to himself*. When he came home, I stuffed down my fears with naïve optimism. I was anxious for life to get back to normal as quickly as possible. I was weary and ragged from parenting alone. I had unraveled in the devastating revelation of the depths and financial repercussions of his addiction. I wanted so badly to just start over and forget the past. I wanted him to find a good job, so he could support our family, which was currently existing on his small unemployment check and the generosity of our families. I didn't want to continue on in this difficult space. *Let's get this addiction thing behind us as fast as we can!*

It was in this season post-rehab that I made huge mistakes as a spouse of a person in recovery. Dave desperately needed help staying clean. No matter how long you're in a controlled rehab environment, as we said in the last chapter, your first ninety days out are critical. He was vulnerable both physically and psychologically to relapse. And what would happen when, not if, he had a migraine again?

In addition, returning to full-time ministry just four months after Dave got out of rehab set him up for a fall. And we can't say we weren't warned. Our pastor at the time was concerned that it was too soon. But the new job at the camp offered the stability I was so desperate for. I believed camp would heal both of us. And Dave was not about to shatter my dreams of normalcy with the truth.

Dave wanted to believe he could manage taking pills for migraines if he just used them as they were prescribed. Rather than adhering to total abstinence, which was my expectation now that he was "healed," he ended up redoubling his efforts at secrecy. Then, as before, he relapsed into pills to manage his stress, and soon he was back to taking thirty pills a day.

Had he been sincere in his repentance? Certainly. But he had become a master of not only deceiving me but deceiving himself. Lies continued to erode our relationship. My reaction when I'd find out I'd been deceived was always anger and hurt. But I wanted so badly for Dave to be trustworthy that, when I stopped being furious with him about money or not picking up the phone when I called, I often returned to trust too quickly. I longed for peace!

When a premature return to trust betrayed me, I turned to the preemptive strike. I hated being surprised, so I tried to stay a step ahead of Dave (as much as I possibly could, with small children to look after). I monitored accounts, called constantly to check on him when he was away from home, quizzed him on where he'd been, and asked him repeatedly whether he was using.

I gave him a million opportunities to lie to me—and he took them. I threw my whole self into preserving our family, my pride, and even to a point, my husband.

Renovating a Marriage

Recovery requires more of a marriage than we think we have left in us. The saying "It gets worse before it gets better" is true when you're attempting to mend a marriage. And when you add issues like finally hearing the whole awful truth (which usually doesn't come out in the first few rounds of conversation), experiencing financial crisis, and the intense discomfort that comes with extended physical withdrawal, the "getting worse" part threatens to break you.

As spouses, we undoubtedly have a long list of valid grievances: *you lied to me, you are not who you say you are, I can't believe anything you say to me, you've made me doubt myself and my own discernment, you've driven us into debt.* We've understandably reached a breaking point. We're so done! We weigh the work involved in restoring a relationship broken by addiction and make decisions based on the history of our relationship with them, or with an ex who was an addict, or on conventional wisdom rather than risk disappointment, devastation, and rejection. And this works both ways, not only for you but for your spouse in recovery as well.

This is why so many marriages end in the wake of addiction.

Rebuilding on Shaky Ground

No one feels the depth and dread of betrayal by your spouse the way you do. Not a pastor, not a parent, not a friend. There's gut-punching, self-denying vulnerability involved in letting a person back into your life who vowed *before God and these witnesses* to honor and cherish you above all else but ended up doing exactly the opposite. Violation of marital trust—not just once but repeatedly—cuts deep.

This destruction of trust leaves shaky ground for rebuilding a marriage. Trust cannot be rebuilt and regained overnight. To willingly put yourself back in a place where you are likely to be hurt again seems foolish to some, and others will never understand how hard it is for you to stay.

Staying together, in the wake of the damage done in addiction, takes extraordinary grace on both sides. And it takes more than that. It's important to find wise counsel who understands that for real healing to take place, for compassion to be renewed, and for real forgiveness to be experienced, injustices between you must be addressed and acknowledged. *Forgive and forget* as a covering for all things is not good counsel for a marriage in recovery from addiction any more than *take two aspirin and call me in the morning* is wise advice for a heart attack. Lying about abusing drugs is not like forgetting to take out the trash again. There's much more to it than that. Forgiveness is hard anytime, but especially when you've been deeply wounded, found grace to forgive, and have been betrayed over and over.

Ask anyone trying to break free from addiction and they will tell you: they've begged God a million times to take their craving away. But when you're on the receiving end of all the apologies, every failure just makes you more skeptical. You've heard "sorry" repeatedly, and yet the cycle continues: *Crash, beg forgiveness, I forgive you, you do okay for a while, you crash, you get caught, you tell me you're sorry.* There's so much up and down and so much to forgive.

Recognizing and Dealing with Shame

I had a lot of expectations about marriage that were created in Bible college. In the first decade or so of our marriage, I thought if I was just an excellent wife, our relationship would be happy. I read every book about my role as a Christian wife that I could get my hands on. I fully believed my obedience to the business of a "godly wife" would be a, if not *the*, major factor in my husband's success. Sometimes, marriage was wonderful, but the migraines and drug dependence inevitably interfered.

I fought a spiritual battle of my own, wrestling out my ideals with God. I had anger, righteous anger over deception. And I didn't know what to do with it. When things got really scary financially, I snapped at Dave and raged and begged and threatened and yelled and sobbed. Conflicts over money turned into threats to leave and a dent in a wall a time or two from a thrown pot.

There weren't a whole lot of Christian advice books out there for women in my place, or if there were, my church library and local bookstore didn't carry them. (This was before Amazon.) So I aspired to follow biblical principles like "win him without a word." Because Dave was not only a Christian but in full-time ministry, I felt like there was no one I could turn to without him losing his job and leaving me and our little ones destitute. I flailed on my own and grabbed hold of anger to survive. I hated my bitterness, and I didn't know what to do with it.

After we moved to Washington, and I finally caught on to Dave's addiction, I gave up on the *good wife* verses in the Bible and embraced a few simple words from Jesus, spoken to me through our pastor's wife the year Dave went to rehab: "If your brother or sister sins against you, rebuke them; and if they repent, forgive them. Even if they sin against you seven times in a day and seven times come back to you saying 'I repent,' you must forgive them."[5] It was all the applicable advice the two of us could find for the situation I was in.

When Dave was in rehab, I considered leaving. But the thought of it broke my heart. I loved him, in spite of the addiction. And I knew he loved me. Call it foolishness, false hope, or wishful thinking, but I decided to stay, because I knew if I left him that consuming, inexplicable enemy addiction would take him away from us.

There's such a fine line between denial and faith, isn't there? Between acknowledging there is a problem and trusting God to work in another person as much as he works in me. *When do you wait? When do you act? What is faith and what is foolishness?*

After we moved to camp, I discovered a relapse every six months. That's about how long he could hide it from me. I gave in to shame again, choosing to bear our problems alone. I tried my own ways to manage, attempting to control as much as I could by handling our finances myself. I prayed daily for Dave to be healed from migraines, and I wanted to believe every relapse was his last. When it wasn't, I was furious.

I asked God to teach me how to love my husband better. I thought maybe all that we were going through was to teach me forgiveness and unfailing love. I compared my attitude and behavior toward Dave to the definition of love in 1 Corinthians 13:

> Love is patient, love is kind. It does not envy, it does not boast, it is not proud. It does not dishonor others, it is not self-seeking, it is not easily angered, it keeps no record of wrongs. Love does not delight in evil but rejoices with the truth. It always protects, always trusts, always hopes, always perseveres.[6]

On the one hand, filtering my attitude and responses to Dave through the biblical definition of love was right. This kind of love can bring real healing. On the other hand, I allowed my own flaws and self-judgment to blind me—not to Dave's sins, but to the severity of the problem. Yes, dealing with addiction calls for love and compassion, but it also calls for practical help. But shame always silenced me.

"Shame needs three things to grow out of control in our lives," writes Brené Brown, "secrecy, silence, and judgment."[7] I was ashamed of Dave's struggle with addiction. And I was ashamed of my reactions to his addiction. This sort of shame-induced silence led to isolation. I didn't break the silence until I recognized that addiction wasn't our only problem. Fighting with Dave about his addiction felt like trying to run in a nightmare. We never, ever really got anywhere and always ended up back in the same horrible place. But the undercurrent of anger was eating away at me, and when it began pouring out on our kids and my friends, it scared me.

Out of desperation for someone to finally hear my silent, seething cries for help, I persuaded Dave to go with me to the pastor at the church we attended after moving from Tacoma to the camp in Poulsbo. Our new pastor referred us to a counselor, whose best help for us was to refer us to a local Celebrate Recovery meeting. (See more about CR in the appendix.)

Discovering a New Community

Everything changed for me when we let the right help into our marriage. Going through the 12 Steps myself helped me see how important it was to talk to someone about our problems. I couldn't believe a roomful of Christians actually gathered together because they had "hurts, habits, and hang-ups." I believe finding that community when we did may have saved our marriage. I know it saved me from myself.

In a Christ-centered recovery group, I finally found a safe space where I could be honest about our problems without risking Dave's job. This relative anonymity and security relieved me of the fear that getting help could do collateral damage to my family, my husband—and even Jesus. I learned that the ways I'd tried to manage Dave's addiction and recovery were not just ineffective and unhealthy but destructive: idle threats and fits of rage did not change him. And the constant suspicion, fear, and attempts to control his behavior had sucked the joy from my life. Something had to change, and I was finally ready and willing to try another way. Working through the steps myself took my focus off my futile attempts to fix Dave and put it on my own issues. Being a watchdog had me angry, stressed, fearful. But through working the steps, I was beginning to let go.

In *The Dance of Anger*, Harriet Lerner writes, "We don't have the power to change another person who does not want to change, and our attempts to do so may actually protect him or her from change."[8] In time, it became clear to me that I needed to let go of Dave's recovery in order for him to really change. But in the recovery process, there was still so much unsettling uncertainty. It was terrifying to give up control.

I had just enough of a taste of freedom through CR that I wanted more. I wanted out of the secrets. But I was so afraid to let go. I was afraid of being poor again, of being homeless. Afraid of the shame of it, and the trauma to our kids. But I knew I couldn't live with secrets anymore. At this point, it was less about trusting Dave and more about trusting God. Ever since Oprah, I had wrestled with opening my hands and fully releasing Dave's recovery to God. It was fear. And it was pride.

I had a turning point that summer when I read John Ortberg's book *Everybody's Normal Till You Get to Know Them*. In it, he retells the story of the woman caught in adultery.[9] The woman's accusers pick up rocks to stone her (under religious law at that time, stoning was the punishment for adultery). Jesus's response to their accusations was, "He who is without sin cast the first stone." While he bent down and wrote in the sand, one by one, the men silently dropped the stones they were holding and walked away.

What got to my heart in Ortberg's retelling of the story was the attention he gave to the accusers:

> All their spiritual power filled them with contempt for the weak. And they became as enslaved by a cold heart as an addict can become enslaved by crack cocaine. What is so insidious about the sins of the spirit is that the carriers don't have a clue. At least with sins of the flesh, you find out you have messed up. With sins of the spirit, you may not even know. You just walk through life with a stone in your hand:

Judgmental thoughts
A superior attitude
Impatient words
Bitter resentments
Little room for love.[10]

Rightness is a language in which I am fluent. And I knew when I read Ortberg's list of sins of the spirit that I was guilty of being judgmental, feeling superior, being impatient, and being bitter toward my husband. My list could go on. When you begin to see your own flaws, let go of legalism, and see yourself as someone in need of mercy for your own failings, you open your heart to extending mercy to others. After years of judging Dave's addiction as a horrible, shameful sin, for the first time I acknowledged it was possible that I might be just as messed up as he was. Just in a different, more culturally acceptable way.

This shift in thought, this new understanding of how God views our faults, gave me reason to hope. I found compassion for Dave again—it had been buried for a while under my own pride and self-protection. Not just sympathy or premature trust that comes and goes, but a conviction that comes from really understanding Dave was loved, deeply loved by Jesus. God was working on Dave just as he was working on me. He was able to handle changing Dave all by himself.

I finally set everything out before God: *Do your will, whatever it takes to heal him.* And I prayed, *God, if he's using, don't let him get away with it.* And then, I let go.

Free Falling

My fragile peace shattered three weeks later. On a dark, rainy day, on the front porch of our house in the woods of the camp, Dave confessed to me that even though he'd been regularly attending CR, he'd relapsed, bought pills again with camp money, and as a result, he had lost his job and our home.

We fell hard, Dave and I. All illusion of security was ripped away in a moment. This was a kick to my gut. And I was right back to angry in a flash. I refused to hear his grief. I rejected his promises of change. For fifteen years I had ridden this roller coaster, and I was finally ready to get off.

But as much as I grieved over these terrible consequences of my husband's addiction and as much as I grieved and raged, I realized he was finally free. And so was I. All the secrets that had bound us for so long were dragged out into the light of day. There was nothing left to hide. No reason to do so. The worst, in my mind, had happened.

This was new. And why, at that pivotal moment, I didn't leave. I stayed to give this whole *recovery* thing a chance.

In those darkest days of our life together after Dave was removed from ministry leadership, God gave me this encouragement through a dear friend: "God is writing an amazing story in Dave's life. Every good story has conflict, tension, and obstacles."

At one time, I had believed God had made Dave for better things—that his life was not going to be wasted by drugs. I'd known Dave since he was nineteen years old. He was the kind of guy in college who could entertain not just a room of people but an audience of a thousand. He was a state debate champion in high school, a gifted communicator, and I knew if he ever really harnessed those powers for good, he would impact the world. But addiction had knocked him off course repeatedly for fifteen years.

I *did* believe God had a far better story for Dave than the one he was living, enslaved to pills. I stayed because I loved Dave. I stayed because I loved my kids and leaving was not going to make their life better. And I stayed because I believed marriage was a sacred agreement unlike any other human relationship.

When we stood before God and made our promises to each other, we made a covenant sealed by ceremony and communion. We walked the aisle between the two sides of our families to the altar to willingly bind ourselves to one another. *The two shall become one flesh, what God has joined together let no man sepa-rate.* "One flesh" sort of blurs the boundary lines.

Nothing will test your endurance like opening your heart again. "Forgiveness," writes Brené Brown, "is so difficult because it in-volves death and grief."[11] Jesus called this "dying to yourself." Dying to self-protection, dying to comfort, dying to an easier path. "Christ did not teach and suffer that we might become, even in the natural loves, more careful of our own happiness," wrote C. S. Lewis.[12] I asked God once again for a love that never gives up but *endures all things, hopes all things, believes all things.* I did not do it perfectly at all. But I believed this wasn't yet the end for us. I believed God could restore us. And I had a white-knuckled grip on hope that he would.

Moving Forward

When I look back, I can see how important it was for Dave to know if he took the tortuous journey through withdrawal and worked hard to change himself, his family would be there at the other end. At the time I just knew I wanted to be there when he turned it around. And to be totally blunt and practical, I didn't want some other woman down the road reaping the benefits of my years of heartache and endurance. We had a long way to go.

Addiction had changed Dave into someone I would never have recognized had I not gone through the slow descent into addiction with him. He was not himself. I was never in physical danger—that's not how Tramadol affected him. He never hit me, never held a gun to my head like some addicts have done. He was a good man. Addiction to pills was his tragic flaw.

The pills flatlined his emotions, and without them, for a time, he was sick and absent from us. It was all he could do to get out of bed and go to work. About eight months into his sobriety, the Dave I married finally reemerged. Over that first year, he physi-cally, mentally, and spiritually came back to life and to himself.

Recovery in our marriage took time. Even after breaking free, we've had some messy, messy years. It's not like a giant reset button was pressed when Dave hit what some would call "rock bottom." It was more like a chasm opened in the earth and parts of us fell into it. There was no way back across it to retrieve what was left on the other side, no way to pull anything that had been lost. There was only forward.

Dave was faced with the choice to either get clean or risk losing his family. And this time, he was willing to do it. Not just the hard work of getting sober, but the humbling work of rebuilding his entire life from the ground up. I saw a glimmer of hope in Dave's humility. He was finally ready to do whatever it took to break free, and I gave him room to work it out . . . without any guarantee that it actually would.

Unbinding a Marriage

⊦DAVE

"When you do not do what you promise," wrote Søren Kierkegaard, "it is a long way back to the truth."[13] Rebuilding trust takes honesty, humility, and accountability. I went from leading a ministry to answering phones as an entry-level counselor in a nonprofit debt counseling call center. Because I was paid hourly, my pay stub showed if I even missed a minute of work. We all knew exactly how long it would take me to get to and from work. In addition, all the debt counselors' calls were recorded, every scrap of paper we used was required to be turned in, and there was no real privacy in my cubicle. If I tried to buy pills online at work, they'd know immediately. All this built-in accountability in my job gave Deb a little peace.

I kept going to weekly recovery meetings, met with our pastor, and checked in regularly with my sponsors from our recovery group. These relationships took even more pressure off Deb. I never went anywhere alone, and absolutely never to a doctor. Deb took over our family finances, what little we had, and our agreement was that I would respond truthfully and kindly to any question she ever asked of me and give her every single receipt for my purchases. This commitment to total transparency gave her the assurance and a little bit of proof that I was being honest. Because of all the years of deception, I knew this was the only way to heal not only our marriage but me.

However, as much as Deb had residual trust issues in recovery, I had them too: *What if I go through all of this and she leaves me anyway?* When you stay together after addiction, you're both taking a chance. Not only that, but in that first year after camp, I was dealing with the reemergence of emotions I had sedated and numbed with drugs for years.

In the middle of conflict, it felt like it was just going to be this way forever—always fighting, never trusted. It was a long time before we had a regular fight over something that didn't feel like it was life or death. In my recovering mind, Deb's anger over something as trivial as my not taking out the trash felt the same as the anger when she caught me taking pills. With every conflict, I felt like *this could be the one that finally ends it.*

Humility for the Long Term

The high level of accountability I had was easier in the first few months of recovery because I felt so much shame. Once I had established some time clean, that's when it became tough, and I had to remind myself why I was submitting to so much accountability. After I started to feel good about myself and where I was in my recovery, that's when we began to have conflict again.

I had to remind myself at times that I'd put Deb through hell. It was going to take a long time for my assurances of honesty to actually mean something. For me, I had to keep in that mode of steady faithfulness, even when I was doing well, because Deb didn't *really* know I was doing well. Part of that was because she'd never been able to tell when I was on Tramadol. She'd only known I'd relapsed when I was caught.

So when I was clean and she had moments of anger and accusations or questioning or suspicion, it hurt. I used to ask her, "What can I do to prove to you that I'm fine?" I'd try to explain to her or convince her that I was being honest, that I wasn't using, and that I really had changed. But I had to let go of trying to prove it with my words.

All of this was different to *me*, but to Deb I was just using the exact same phrases and tone of voice as I had when it was a lie. In moments when I expressed my frustration with Deb's obvious distrust, she found ways to firmly articulate, "I'm still here, but how dare you be mad about this." Or, "I'm still in pain about this."

Somewhere along the way, I realized I was never going to convince Deb by how I acted or what I said. There was nothing I could do other than just stay clean. Only time would tell. That's how I proved myself. I had to adjust my expectations and realize trust was not going to be rebuilt this time in a month, or even a year.

You can't make time go faster. In those first days of me being clean, Deb and I used to talk about how we wished it was a year from now or ten years from now, just so proving my sobriety would be done, so we could both know for sure it was real. But there was no quick way to get ten years down the road into rebuilt trust. You just have to live through each day. We both had to accept that the discomfort was going to stay for a long time. We had to have compassion for each other in the middle of it. I had to work to show compassion for Deb's suspicion and fear and doubt, even when I knew I was being completely honest.

That whole first year was rough. Over-the-top accountability and humility were required in those early years of recovery in order to save our marriage. I had men in my life who were saying, *This is a consequence of the years of lies. Of course she's still suspicious, of course you should show her that receipt*, or *Just allow for her to look at you funny and not be offended by it.*

When I'd meet one of my sponsors or my pastor for coffee, Deb would check in with a call and ask to speak with the person I was meeting, just to ease her mind that I was doing what I said I was doing. (Lying about where I was had been a pattern for a long, long time.) I gladly gave them the phone to say "hi" and prove where I was. Sometimes it took me a while to come around to see how valid her need for assurance was and to stay humble. And sometimes, I had to draw on a not-so-noble internal motivation of *She's going to eat these words in six months.*

When I meet with guys in recovery from addiction now, I ask, "What can you do to show that you're really committed to change?" If you really are willing to do whatever it takes to save your relationship, you're going to have to stay in that place of humility longer than you wish—until your spouse believes the change.

Once the trust began to come back, at least for me and my personality, I found that trust was a much better deterrent than being in trouble. For fifteen years I had been "in trouble." But once I got a taste of real trust, *and was actually worthy of it*, I wanted to see that grow. I didn't want to throw it away and start over again. Just like I didn't want to go through acute withdrawal again.

Hard Work and Humility

Dave endured a lot of scrutiny, distrust, and even some belligerence from me that first full year of his sobriety. I was deeply wounded and afraid of trusting him again. I was right not to trust him yet, but I could give him room to grow. He knew the only way to mend our relationship—and stay sober—was if he lived an open and transparent life from that point on. No secrets. What I asked of Dave required an extraordinary level of humility on his part. And he was willing to do it. I did not have to force him to tell me things anymore.

So many marriages riddled with addiction issues end right here. If your spouse in recovery is not willing to humble themselves and work hard—for as long as it takes—to regain your trust after lying to you for years, you probably won't stay married long. *Heavy-duty, life-changing accountability requires humility.*

On the other hand, in order to preserve and rebuild your marriage relationship, you cannot be your spouse's recovery accountability partner or sponsor. You're not responsible to make sure your spouse is showing up to meetings or being a good employee. Someone else needs to take that role. This is a hard transition if you've been holding your spouse accountable for a long time. That's why support from people who've been through it themselves can be a lifeline.

Healing a marriage damaged by drug addiction is a process. We can never lose sight of that. If we do, we can easily fall into a relapse of our own, right back into controlling habits, fear, and the crazy cycle. Dave's steady faithfulness strengthened my hope, and in turn my belief and hope encouraged his faithfulness. And our new community kept us from going back to managing and hiding.

—⊣{ DAVE —

You can't rush recovery, even if your spouse is finally drug free. Grace allows them to just survive for a while. When we finally accepted that the process was going to take years instead of months, we decided to use the time in front of us to heal our family. Our kids needed our love and attention. They needed healthy parents. Away from ministry, we were able to give ourselves some space to work things out in our marriage without pressure. There was no rush to get back into ministry or to lead an organization.

Deb made my recovery a priority. She wasn't just supportive, she knew it was necessary. I remember at least once telling Deb, "I don't want to go to recovery group tonight," and her saying calmly, "Well, I can't make that decision for you, but I'm going." And she did. At group, we both had people we could turn to and express our frustration about where things were with us, people who helped us continue to move forward from the past.

I've never been super observant, but she didn't chew me out for not noticing what needed to be done around dinnertime when I got home from work. Especially when I was still in withdrawal and barely holding it together through a workday. I'd get home and sit in a hot bath and try to relax before joining the family. My anxiety in withdrawal was so high, I couldn't handle the chaos. Her patience and compassion was fueled by a commitment to real recovery.

Taking Steps toward Healing

How we treat our spouse in recovery influences their sobriety. Support at this stage is key. It's critical that your spouse finds the recovery path that is right and possible for them. Find a way to make it work and prioritize their recovery. Is it counseling? Is it a 12 Step meeting? Don't ask them to skip and stay with the kids so you can go to the movies with your friends. Are they in the critical first ninety days off pills? Drop them off at their meetings. Or better, find someone you trust to watch the kids and go to a meeting of your own once a week. And get support and health for yourself, including counseling.

Support them when they're doing the right things. Pray continuously and specifically. Write down your specific prayers. Celebrate when those prayers are answered. Notice. Take joy in positive progress. Are they holding down a job now when they weren't before? That's progress!

It's probably too much to ask your spouse in recovery to notice what needs to be done around the house—especially if for years they've been disconnected. But when you need help, be specific and kind. Try something like, "Hey, honey, can you please take the kids into the backyard and throw the ball around a bit while I finish making dinner?" Or "Can you chop up the rest of these veggies while I feed the baby?" If they respond negatively to kindness, that's their choice, and your gentle answer will keep things calm. If they're in a recovery program, encourage them to talk with their sponsor about conflicts.

It's not unreasonable to expect our spouse in recovery to help, but out of enthusiasm and desperation for things to be normal, we are often prone to expect too much. Taking a leap from being strung out on drugs to Super Dad or Wonder Mom is unrealistic. Those expectations set them up for failure.

Practice honesty and kindness. Be positive. Stop *expecting* failure. Even with his commitment to total honesty, it was much easier for Dave to respond positively if I wasn't acting angry. If *I* wasn't mad, *he* didn't get mad.

Protect their recovery. If your spouse is an alcoholic, how loving is it for you to continue drinking in front of them while they are breaking free? If your spouse struggles with pill addiction, don't leave prescriptions around when you have to take them. Empty your medicine cabinets, your liquor cabinet. If you love them, you can learn to do without your glass of wine with dinner or the Vicodin you keep just in case.

Protect your marriage. At low points when I was younger, I fantasized about what it would be like to be married to someone who didn't struggle with addiction. I'm old enough now to have seen relationships I idealized fall apart. Accept that your marriage is not and will not be perfect, not because of your spouse or yourself but because no marriage is.

Respect privacy but give yourself safe spaces to speak freely with a counselor, support group, and trusted friend. Think carefully before sharing publicly about their addiction and ask their permission; find a friend, counselor, and/or support group with whom you can share without reservation. Practice discernment. Look carefully at the bias, experience, and worldview of the person giving advice.

Don't take your stress out on the kids, and don't get them—or any family members—involved in your conflicts (unless you're asking them to help you get out of an abusive situation). Taking sides can happen so quickly, and it's not fair to anyone.

Give it time. Sometimes we write people off just when they're turning around. And like in any other form of recovery—a surgery, an injury, grief—it takes time to heal. Not just days but weeks, months, and—depending on the severity—years! Forgiveness that leads to reconciliation may come slowly. It's a delicate balance between the recovering addict's faithfulness and our compassion. It took two years of faithful, honest, open living from Dave for me to trust him again. Two years!

They say when we're grieving the loss of a spouse that we should not make significant life changes for a year. What if we gave healing from addiction the sort of time we give grief? Restoring our marriage, family, and life has taken years. For eleven years now, Dave has taken one step at a time in the right direction, and we've been rebuilding our home, faithful in little to faithful in much.

Work genuinely toward trusting again and learn to practice grace and kindness. Begin to believe the best, and your broken marriage may begin to heal. Dave is not who he once was, and neither am I. We are proof of miracles.

Recovery in Community

Please remember that you don't have to do any of this alone. I know that as hard as it was to have our life ripped out from under us,

Dave's openness about his addiction was exactly what we needed in order for our marriage, and for me, to heal. It invited others in and gave me freedom to stay in our relationship and get the help and support I needed. Not everyone who has struggled with addiction is so open. No one who needs help really wants it announced online or in a prayer request or pastoral visit. The rest of this book goes into detail about how powerful a supportive community can be for someone in addiction recovery, but this need for community is also true for you as their spouse. More than a book, you need community.

As I mentioned earlier, I am not a counselor or therapist, and if you are in an abusive situation, please get the help you need from a qualified professional. But I will tell you what made it possible for me to stay in our marriage. We had support—people in our life who were not going to let us live on the streets. Our recovery group, accountability partners, sponsors, our church—they all had, in big and small ways, a part in healing our marriage. We had a community that was willing to learn to help us mend.

four

The Support of Family

> To love a person means to see him as God intended him to be.
>
> FYODOR DOSTOEVSKY

> Do not hide from relatives who need your help.
>
> ISAIAH 58:7

In his bestselling book *Hillbilly Elegy*, J. D. Vance writes about his childhood growing up in Southern Ohio in the on-again, off-again care of his Kentucky hills–born grandparents and drug-addicted mother. Families who've been through a long battle with addiction know that Vance's story is not unique. It could be the story of any child raised by a parent in addiction.

The beauty in Vance's story, however, is a truth we've seen everywhere—in interviews I've done with those in rescue missions and prison ministries, in our church, and in our own family. Behind every miraculous transformation is someone who never gave up.

Vance credits his tough-as-nails "Mamaw" for his successes in life. She picked up the pieces when Vance's mother was in and out of relationships and high on drugs. But his grandparents didn't have to break the relationship between their daughter and her children to do it. They were a rough-around-the-edges sort of family, but for the most part, as Vance tells it, his grandparents were able to both care for him and show compassion for his mom even when they had to step into his life to take her place.

This is a delicate balance for a loving grandparent. How do you keep your precious grandchildren safe from an unsafe parent while practicing kindness and compassion toward your son or daughter who *is* that unsafe parent? How do you do this with a broken heart?

In the past decade, the number of grandparents who are bringing up their grandchildren because their kids are on drugs, in prison, or trying to get their lives back together in recovery has exploded. Generations United's 2016 report *Raising the Children of the Opioid Epidemic* examines the effect the crisis has had on families: "With the rise in heroin and other opioid use, more relatives are raising children because the parents have died, are incarcerated, are using drugs, are in treatment or are otherwise unable to take care of their children."[1] In other words, if you have custody of or are caring for your grandkids or nieces or nephews—you're not alone. Families all over the country are doing the same thing.

Maybe it's generational, and maybe it's just how you were raised, but some families are tight-knit and will bend over backward to help each other. Our parents, Dave's and mine, are all givers when it comes to family. We have been blessed by them throughout our marriage. And we have extended family who love relentlessly as well. One of Dave's uncles said in his eulogy at a recent family funeral, "This family never gives up on people."

Love and acceptance are the strengths of a good family. And family relationships are a vital component of nurture and growth. That's the beauty—and the pain—of family. We are permanently connected to each other. And good families are the first line of care when a family member is struggling.

Everywhere a person in crisis goes for help, they'll be asked the same question: *Do you have any family members who can help?* But families who have suffered through years of their loved one's erratic behavior in addiction are understandably reluctant at times to help their "prodigal."

Fears of "enabling," fears of getting hopes up only to be disappointed—there's a path of suffering for someone who has loved an addict. So when it comes to the next hard step—walking beside your loved one through recovery—you need a renewed vision and hope. The journey through recovery may be long, but we have a guide through it. God's relationship to his chosen people is a beautiful example of balancing consequences and compassion. Even when God was angry over disobedience, his love was enduring. Consider Lamentations 3:31–32: "For no one is cast off by the Lord forever. Though he brings grief, he will show compassion, so great is his unfailing love."

The Father's Compassion

When God is referred to in Scripture as "our Father," we're meant to understand the relationship to be a tender and loving one. Psalm 103:13 says, "Just as a father has compassion on his children . . ." And Isaiah 49:15: "Can a mother forget the baby at her breast and have no compassion on the child she has borne?"

Compassion is supposed to be an innate response to our children. When they break our hearts, however, hardening our hearts with anger feels better than living with the pain. It's excruciating to keep a tender heart toward a child who continuously breaks it. Yes, there were consequences for the children of Israel when they strayed from the path, but God's love for them was so great, his heart so broken for their inability to get things right, that he came to us in the form of a child, grew into a man, and suffered and died to mend the broken relationship.

Jesus embodied the Father's compassion for us, and he expected compassion to be our response to those who disappoint us. When Jesus taught about grace for sinners in Luke 15, he used lost-and-found stories to drive his message home. In the example of the lost sheep, Jesus says *of course* you would leave the ninety-nine to go search for the lost one. When a woman loses a full day's wages by dropping a coin somewhere in her house, *of course* she will search for it till it's found. And when a child has wandered away and broken your heart, squandering everything you've ever given him, *of course* when he comes home, you will celebrate. *Welcome home, prodigal.* Dad doesn't even wait for an explanation. While he was still a long way off, his father saw him coming. Filled with love and compassion, he ran to his son, embraced him, and kissed him.[2]

The Father's compassion for us means we don't have to earn his love as his children. His love is long-suffering. He is kind. He is patient with us. And when we come back to him, he won't turn us away.[3]

How we welcome our children when they're abusing drugs or alcohol can be a door to their recovery, but it will, in many cases, present a complicated path, particularly if the safety of others is a concern. In *Beautiful Boy*, a memoir of a father's unwavering love for his child, David Sheff's love and support for his son endures through rehab and relapse and another try at rehab, and then relapse again and again. Instead of cutting Nic out of his life completely, he models the endurance of the love a parent should have for their child. But Sheff comes to understand that as much as he loves his drug-abusing son, Nic, he also must protect his other children, Jasper and Daisy. He can't allow Nic to use illegal drugs and keep drug paraphernalia in their home, so Nic has to leave.

The trouble with human parents is that we aren't perfect. We're going to make mistakes. We've exploded when the most helpful response would have been a calm conversation. We've ignored signs when we were afraid to know the truth. We've carried our own adverse life experiences and pains into our relationships with our children: fears, shame, all of it. And in a crisis like a child's addiction, our own hurts have boiled to the surface. As parents, we've turned on each other and hurled blame. We've been angry. We don't sleep. We've been obsessed with trying to fix our loved one. We've said things we wish we could take back. We let the phone calls and texts go unanswered.

Even though our son or sister or dad is no longer abusing drugs—which is a reason to rejoice—damage has been done. Repairing it takes time. In recovery, there is plenty of mending work to do for family members. The closer we are to the addict, the more our loved one's recovery work will eventually involve us, and we likely have some recovery work to do ourselves. Just like in a marriage relationship, we may have significant and critical changes to make. We need to acknowledge our own issues independent of our loved one's issues. There's a temptation to slip back into denial and tell ourselves everything is fixed, but remember, this is just the beginning of restoration.

Allowing Recovery to Be Incremental

—{ DAVE —

Among the families I've worked with over the years, a common frustration stems from expectations and misunderstanding about what recovery is. Detox, rehab, and recovery are all very different, but many people use them interchangeably. *Detox* is the physical act of getting clean. *Rehab* is either an inpatient or outpatient program. *Recovery* is learning how to live again without falling back into your addiction.

We expect getting clean and sober to change everything. They come out of rehab and everyone looks at them and thinks, "Oh, you're off drugs, you're fixed." Whether your family member goes to a weekend in inpatient detox, a week in jail, three weeks in rehab, or a year on a ranch, you want them to come out a new person. You want them to be who they used to be before drugs. Or better yet, maybe they'll be a better person than they were before.

The hope and goal you have for a loved one is total victory. It's hard to accept small steps as real changes. Changing our expectation from one giant, all-encompassing transformation to steps (growth sliced thin) gives hope to everyone. Failure on a small step is less devastating than a total collapse. You're more likely to climb back up from slipping off the curb than you are from falling off the house. Success in small steps gives confidence to take big steps.

We've already said recovery can be a slow process. Your relationship with your loved one in recovery from addiction requires as much prayer, patience, and walking in faith as it did when they were active in addiction and you prayed for their release. It doesn't stay this way forever. This is just a transition.

Your loved one may feel like nothing will ever be good in their life again; reviving can be difficult. They are growing into their sobriety, and they have so much to deal with. First and foremost, living without the drug they turned to for help.

Start looking for the good. Maybe they came back and apologized for snapping at you in the morning. Or they showed initiative by doing something on their own. Take these as positive steps and remember that, especially at first, each step is agony for them. There were days in early recovery (the first ninety days) that I told myself, "Just make it through the next fifteen minutes." I couldn't think beyond that. I just had to make it through.

A few months into the process, everyone wants recovery to just be over . . . but like grief and loss (for the addict, in a strange way, it *is* loss) it will be different. The drugs masked some sort of pain, whether it was physical or psychological. They may go through depression. There's a lot going on. It may not look at all like you'd hoped.

If we're encouraged only when our loved one in recovery is excited about recovery, it produces again the idea that they have to pretend everything is great and happy. But that's not how God the Father expects us to behave when we are hurting. God wants us honest—as we are, where we are. And progress, even (especially) slow progress, is preferable to false and external change. Expecting "fixed" is asking for something external. We all need inner change that is deep and real and enabled by God. That's what's happening here: deep inner change. Loving your family member in recovery right where they are is important. And remember, they will still have normal difficulties and faults just like you do. Not everything about them can be attributed to their addiction. Their insecurities, their forgetfulness, a bit of temper—allowing them to have normal human failings, just like you do, is grace.

———————

Helping or Hurting

The question continually before those walking alongside a recovering addict is, "Am I helping or hurting?" Families play a powerful role in addiction recovery, but family relationships also have the potential to be a stumbling block. In their book *Understanding and Loving a Person with Alcohol or Drug Addiction*, Stephen Arterburn and Dr. David Stoop write, "The addicted person you love may feel very alone, but the truth is, her problem is really a family problem, and treatment and recovery is a family affair as well. That means you are part of the solution that will lead to recovery and healing."[4]

While recovering addicts need to own their own recovery, they also need encouragement and support. This is a hard spot for family. The closer we are, the harder it gets. We get caught between what is helping and what is enabling—and maybe we're not even sure what *enabling* means. How do we believe the best of them and still be wise? How much do we let them feel and bear the painful consequences of their choices? And how do we know when they desperately need a hand? As in, this time the money they need *really is* for rent and not drugs, like before.

Many of us need important reminders about where we end and where another person begins, but like any other principle, boundaries can become selfish and even a form of legalism. Like the overly strict parenting philosophies some of us attempted to implement when our kids were little, overapplication and misapplication of relationship advice can carry us far off the path of Christlike love for our loved one and from being ministers of God's love to our families. What I find missing in so many guides is the Father's heart of compassion: the mercy that suffers along with us. When someone we love is suffering, even if their suffering is self-inflicted, it will hurt us. It's supposed to. Compassion is not comfortable, nor is it secure. It requires vulnerability, and it costs us. Compassion draws us closer to their pain. We can't protect ourselves from being hurt.

Overfunctioning or Boundaries

Boundaries are a conversational minefield. The invisible lines we draw between ourselves and another person define responsibility. We have to be cautious and prayerful about line drawing, because there are times when our boundaries may actually be more about our own character flaws and personal comfort zones than they are about helping the person we're drawing a boundary line with.

People who are really good at "setting boundaries" with others are sometimes *too* good at it. So good, in fact, that they rarely do anything inconvenient or promise to do something they know is going to cost them emotionally or financially—even for family. This misapplication of boundaries is why in this context I prefer Harriet Lerner's use of the term *overfunctioning*. Overfunctioning means habitually doing for someone what they are able to do for themselves.

It's true that families can be the biggest violators of good "boundaries," because they develop habits of overfunctioning for underfunctioning household members. Parents of adult children who are in or recovering from addiction often struggle with over-functioning for their son or daughter.

If your child (or parent or sibling) is married, and you want them to stay that way, it's important to respect their relationship. Overfunctioning for them can cause problems between the one in recovery and their spouse and do damage to a marriage at any time, but when a marriage is as fragile as it often is in recovery, the potential for damage is exponential. There is a point where recovery is impacting their spouse more than it's affecting you as their parent. That makes it their problem to solve. Your interference, no matter how kindly intended, can quickly enable your child to continue in their underfunctioning ways and drive a wedge between them and their spouse. If the spouse has determined they will not overfunction for the person in recovery and you don't understand it, talk to them directly, not through the addict, if at all possible.

Here are some good examples of parents respecting marriage boundary lines:

- Protect their dignity by not asking for prayer for them or making vague comments on social media.
- Don't agree to keep secrets for the person in addiction (e.g., "Please don't tell my husband you gave me this money") unless there is danger of retribution like physical abuse (in the case of physical abuse, seek counsel and safety).
- Be careful about giving advice that pertains more to healthier marriages. Instituting a regular date night or going to a weeklong marriage retreat isn't going to make it all better. Addiction complicates a marriage relationship.
- Encourage marriage counseling when you encounter resistance rather than pushing hard for forgiveness and reconciliation. You do not know what went on behind closed doors. They may not be telling you everything.

Be aware that, as parents, your disrespect of a marriage in recovery can have a harmful, even destructive, influence.

People who are in recovery are peeling back layers to get to the heart of their struggle. Sometimes when the unraveling of the mummy begins, it gets ugly. Some days we're flooded with compassion, other days we're skeptical of their sincerity and question their sobriety. If we're not anchored, we're tossed on the waves of emotional reaction, but for both personalities, and everyone in between, most of the time, when the person struggling with addiction is someone you love, you always wonder if you're doing the right thing.

This place requires prayer, thoughtfulness, and flexibility, and it's a nightmare for people who love plans and like the way clearly mapped out for them. The temptation for map-oriented people is to depend on a formula like if/then: *If he does this, then I will do this.* We want a plan of action. We want contracts and guarantees. But even for those of us who are far more comfortable with a little uncertainty, our flexibility will be stretched and tested in addiction recovery in ways we never imagined. In essence, we're fighting for some control over the chaos their former behavior created in our lives.

This uncertainty keeps us at the feet of Jesus, praying for wisdom, discernment, and compassion. Remember how God deals with us, how he loves us, how he doesn't slam the door on us.

Examining Ourselves

For family members, one of the most difficult parts of addiction recovery is examining ourselves and being willing to look at whether, and how, we might have contributed to the problem. I know how hard this was for me as a wife. Though I've had limited experience accompanying a family member to a counselor's office, I can tell you, it was *the worst*. If you're like me, no one could possibly be harder on you than you are on yourself—but that experience in a counselor's office comes close. Recovery group was a much more gentle place to learn.

—⊣| DAVE—

The interesting thing we don't hear in Christian communities where addiction is strictly labeled as a "sin" is that there may be a reason for addiction that isn't just about rebellion or rejection of God or even bad choices. Underneath all "vices" is an attempt to fill a void that could be caused by anything from a learning disability to finding acceptance with the wrong crowd.

As we grow up, we become responsible for ourselves. An addict's choices are theirs. People become addicted to drugs for a reason, but in *A Hunger for Healing,* J. Keith Miller says addiction is about "covering our intense pain so we don't have to feel it."[5] When that cover is removed, we're still left with pain, whether it's physical, mental, or relational. Even when an addiction starts with a prescription, like a bottle of Vicodin for back surgery, the motive for abusing it may have been to get that carefree feeling again when something painful happens.

A drug relieves the pain of social discomfort. It feels dependable—it's always there and it will work every time. It is easy—no need to accomplish something to feel good. It's pleasure—not joy, not even happiness. It is unconditional. It feels controllable. It made me feel outgoing, likable, and safe. Oh, and it also made physical pain, my migraines, go away.

———— ||—

Acknowledging Past Trauma

Sometimes drugs or alcohol are the means to numb memories of serious trauma. When our child is the victim, it's difficult enough to acknowledge that they may have had trauma, and it's hard to deal with traumas they've had that we know nothing about.

The Adverse Childhood Experiences (ACE) Survey gathered data from 17,000 Kaiser Permanente patients in the 1990s to study the lingering impact of childhood trauma. In the initial study, "adverse childhood experiences" were defined as abuse, domestic violence, substance abuse in the home, mental illness in the home, parental separation or divorce, incarceration of a family member, and neglect. The study found that the higher the ACE score, meaning the more of these things they've experienced, the more likely the subject was to struggle with addiction.[6]

Recognizing the suffering at the root of addiction can lead us to greater compassion. However, if the one struggling with addiction is our child, a sense of shame and failure may rise up in us—even when we weren't the cause. We may feel like we let our child down by not protecting them from trauma. We can't bring ourselves to talk about it. We react to conversations about it with our own response to trauma, whether that's to fight it, run away from it, or shut down.

Your loved one may have some deep, deep wounds. They may have things to tell you that you wish you didn't have to hear. I know these things are hard to talk about, and depending on the depth of the wound, it could be years before they are able to tell you the whole story. What's important to remember is that our denial doesn't help—"you can't heal a wound by saying it's not there."[7] Getting a family counselor involved can help you through this process, and so can finding a good support group. Support groups are free and available worldwide and will help you realize you are not alone.

Supporting Recovery

—*H*DAVE—

As a family member starts recovery, learning more about the recovery process can help us encourage them and be supportive. This may entail some adjustments to expectations. We will have to deal with our assumptions and any unhealthy ways we dealt with their addiction and its side effects. (This is part of our own recovery process.) It can be so healing for our loved one when we acknowledge where we may have gotten it wrong and ask their forgiveness. Our tenderheartedness—not weakness, but kindness—can spark change. It's also freeing to stop blaming ourselves for their choices. All of us are in need of grace and mercy.

In recovery, we've seen families reexamine their presuppositions and ideas about what addiction is, what recovery is, and how all of it works in order to encourage and support their adult child's recovery. Again, recovery takes time. And it takes cooperation.

Here are a few common ways we see families help and hinder the recovery process.

Willingness to see recovery as a process, not a onetime event, helps the recovery process.

Leona firmly believes addiction is a sin. If her adult son, Tony, would just repent, he would be free from his pill addiction. Leona set up an intervention involving family members. Tony broke down and confessed to the family that he's begged God for help, pleaded with him to remove the pull toward temptation, but can't seem to break free. The whole family prayed over Tony. Tony prayed. Everyone in the family believed he was set on a new path.

And then Tony's father caught him sneaking pills from their medicine cabinet—again. Tony's parents were heartbroken. They told him he was *living in sin* and asked the other family members not to see him again until he repented fully and changed. This was what Leona and her husband were taught in Bible college. They heard it on a family program on the radio too. They were practicing *tough love*.

But Tony took pills because he felt like he couldn't do his job without them. Rejection and failure are his biggest fears. Tony continued to go to his 12 Step group and, after a few months, invited his parents. For the sake of their son, Leona and her husband were willing to investigate the 12 Steps and their foundation on biblical principles. They've admitted to their son that they don't understand how he can be a Christian and still struggle, so they've found a support group for parents of addicts and are learning how to walk through recovery beside him now, rather than reject him until he has his life back together.

Believing the "right" program will fix the problem hinders the recovery process.

Jenna doesn't know much about addiction, but she's desperate because her forty-year-old sister Lori's life has spiraled out of control. She did a little research and, based on a recommendation from a friend who had some success with a ninety-day inpatient rehab, Jenna found a Christ-based program that makes some great promises. It's expensive, but Lori needs serious help, so Jenna is willing to pay. Jenna and her brother stage an intervention with the help of a counselor and they persuade Lori to go.

But Lori stayed in the center less than twenty-four hours before she called a friend to pick her up. The tens of thousands of dollars Jenna and her brother paid are not refundable because the guarantee of success is only for those who *complete* the program.

As difficult as it is to acknowledge, Jenna and her brother can't force recovery. The slap of intervention might have woken Lori up, but it may take several of these types of experiences to get her to take action. An intervention may have gotten her to acknowledge she has a problem and the fact that she has hurt people, is hurting herself, and is on a downward spiral. But she may not be ready to quit. Interventions *can* have the opposite of the intended effect, especially for someone who already feels hopeless. If they fail to stick with the program, they may feel they've let you down so much you could never forgive them.

Though an inpatient program might be the way to break through to someone trapped in addiction, the reality is that adults aren't required to stay against their will unless it's court-ordered. (Sometimes, court-ordered is effective.) Releasing the outcome and letting God deal with someone you love is one of the hardest things for a close family member to do. Even though Jenna's sister is the one with the problem, a support group like Al-Anon or Celebrate Recovery can be a source of support for Jenna and her other family members. She'll meet other families whose hearts ache because of a loved one's addiction, and over time, she'll forge strong, supportive relationships.

Lori's in recovery now and her program looks nothing like what her sister thought it should. She ended up in jail and is now in a sober living home where she has ongoing, daily encouragement to stay clean.

Accepting relapse as a part of change salvages the recovery process.

Ben's alcoholic father, Stephen, completed a nine-month Christian residential recovery program, and everyone thought he was doing well. But within a few months, the new life they celebrated with their church seemed to have evaporated. He got hired by a friend of the family and then lost the job for not showing up. He started fighting with his new wife again. She kicked him out, and Ben took him in.

One night Stephen opened up to his son and told him how hard it was for him to adjust to life outside the program and how hard it was not to be allowed to go home. A few weeks later, in the middle of an argument with Ben about some beer bottles in the trash, Stephen broke down and admitted to drinking again to make it through the day. Ben was angry and the situation felt hopeless again. Should his father go back into the program? It worked once, maybe it would work again?

Stephen was ready for change, but he worried that going into another residential program would only drive a wedge further between him and his wife, with whom he wants to reconcile. Through a friend, Stephen found a counselor who specializes in addiction recovery. The counselor is addressing the reasons he turns to alcohol, and with his help, Stephen is learning to deal with the ups and downs of life without it. He got a job with flexibility to attend meetings and counseling, not just for him, but with his wife as well. After a brief separation, they are together again and working toward restoration.

Educating Ourselves

As we've said, the process of recovery looks different for everyone. Not everyone who is addicted to drugs gets to the point where they've made an obvious shambles of their life. While there is an observable pattern or path addiction follows and recovery takes in people's lives, the downward spiral or upward climb may be slower or faster and some of the signs may not apply.

In the mid-twentieth century, E. Morton Jellinek observed and recorded the progression of alcoholism, known as the Jellinek curve (see the chart in the appendix). The bottom of the curve is often referred to as "rock bottom," but we now know it's not always true that a person struggling with addiction has to hit the bottom to bounce back up. (For tens of thousands of people each year, rock bottom is death.) The chart can be a helpful resource for understanding the process, as long as we remember that recovery is personal and the stages may be different. Also, not everyone in legitimate recovery is in a 12 Step program.

No matter what your relationship is to your loved one in re-covery, educating yourself about addiction and recovery will help tremendously. Support what they're doing to break free, but read widely, because there are all kinds of opinions, theories, and programs. Beware of the authors and programs that claim huge success rates and that purport their method is the "proven effective" way. From TV and radio shows, we get the idea that recovery looks like intervention, rehab, restoration. But that's not necessarily true. If you dig deep into a recovery program, you'll find it was founded by someone who built it on what worked for *them*.

Resist "one best way" thinking. No matter how much we love the person caught in addiction or how much tough love we dole out or how firm we are with our boundaries, none of it will change them if they aren't ready to yield.

I've had the same conversation over and over for a decade now. Loved ones come seeking advice for dealing with their adult child's addiction. I'm always willing to meet with the son or daughter (if they're willing), but as gently as I can, I tell them the thing they don't want to hear: *You can't fix it*. You can pray. You can love. You can welcome. You can keep your eyes open and *be wise as serpents and harmless as doves*.

The addict's willingness to meet may result in nothing, or it may open the door just a crack. I get calls all the time from people I met with a year or two or five before. At that time, they were meeting to comply with their loved one's request. Now, they're ready to try to get clean. Keep praying. Keep loving. Show compassion. *Don't give up hope*.

Recovery Can Be Complicated

As I pulled the pieces of this chapter together, our hearts were buried with a dozen boys and their soccer coaches trapped in a flooded cave in Thailand. And I couldn't help but think of how well their predicament illustrates the agony of a family going through addiction recovery.

The team was exploring caves when flooding forced them farther into the tunnels in search of higher ground. After nine days

The Role of a Parent of a Minor Struggling with Addiction

When your child is a teenager caught up in drugs or alcohol, you may be their greatest lifeline for help. Vigilance and intervention may save their life, and specialized recovery programs can get them through the dangerous days and years. There are numerous books written about fighting to free a son or daughter from addiction, and you can find a list of them in the appendix of this book. As a parent of someone in, or recovering from, addiction, consider your own need for the community of other parents who've been through, or are going through, the same thing. Find community in a local church, get involved in a support group.

Disagreements about parenting escalate when we're dealing with a problem as charged as addiction. Finding some sort of common ground between you may strain everything you and your spouse have, but it's the place to begin. If you can't find agreement, a counselor can be a tremendous help and save your marriage. You may be asking, "Why should I go to a counselor when my kid is the one with the problem?" Because their addiction affects you too, probably more than you know. At times our response to the shortcomings of another person is personality-driven

of intense rescue operations, the news spread around the world in seconds: *Found Alive!*

But joy gave way in the morning to the terrible news that they wouldn't be pulled from the cave anytime soon. I think the whole world may have groaned at once in collective claustrophobia when officials predicted it could take them four months to get them out.

"This is going to be a complicated rescue," the experts said.[8] The boys were two miles into the caves and more than a half mile underground. The cavern they were in was only accessible through a narrow, dark, muddy, flooded channel. It was the rainy season in Southeast Asia, and the caves refilled with water as fast as it was pumped out of them.

rather than truth-driven. And our personality-driven responses can do a lot of damage.

Misconceptions can keep parents of children caught in addiction from seeking help. It's a normal response for parents to wonder if their child's struggle has anything to do with them as a parent. We may know what we did. There are times we own up to it, but there are also times we're afraid to give an inch lest the whole thing suddenly become *our fault*. It's painful to acknowledge that addiction doesn't happen in a vacuum, that something inside our child, no matter their age, was or is broken enough that they're trying to fix it with pills, drugs, alcohol, or whatever numbs them. Maybe something happened in childhood, maybe it happened later, but there is no such thing as a perfect parent, and our failures, quirks, and sins are passed on in some form to our children, no matter how hard we resist. It's also possible that a struggle has nothing to do with us at all. Sometimes kids make choices they haven't thought through and the consequences are devastating.

The teen years are especially fragile when it comes to drugs, and enlisting the help of professionals is critical, not only for you, but also for your child.

Ideas for rescue operations included drilling into the cavern or teaching the boys to scuba dive. Both options were considered extremely dangerous. A diver even died attempting to rescue them. There was no safe way out.

The parents of these children stood by helplessly as experts did everything they knew how to do to bring their children to safety. There was nothing the parents could do personally to hurry the rescue process along. They couldn't swim into the cave to grab their children. They couldn't dig down and pull them out themselves. They had to trust the rescue process to God and the skilled workers and volunteers who came from all over the world.

The news of four more months of waiting would have devastated me as a parent. My breath is sucked away just thinking of it. On one hand, *Thank you, Father, they've been found.* On the other, *Lord, have mercy!* Waiting is so awful. But what choice did they have? Can you imagine if the parents had walked away saying, "What's the use? There's no chance of getting them all out alive," while so many were working around the clock on their behalf?

The news stations revived past stories of people trapped underground: Baby Jessica trapped in a well, thirty-three Chilean miners buried in a collapsed mine shaft. Although their stories are all about being rescued from the bowels of the earth, the details of each rescue are very different. Every "buried alive" situation is nuanced. No divers were called for Baby Jessica. In Chile, a man-sized capsule was sent through a half-mile tunnel to pull the miners out one at a time. In the end, in Thailand, each of the boys was brought out of the cave on a stretcher guided by two divers. It took the first team eight hours to make the trip out of the cave with the first group of boys. More days of an agonizing wait . . .

Recovery, like the rescue in Thailand, is complicated. It might take many different tries, different teams, different programs. But don't give up.

Family support is the number one factor in successful, sustained recovery from addiction.[9] We may not have a "hands-on role," but that doesn't mean we are giving up. We can encourage, pray, assist, and love them with kindness and gentleness. We can find support and call professionals. We can find encouragement. The comfort in the recovery process is this: we don't have to go through it alone.

five

Friendship in Recovery

> Even when we forsake the fear of God, we need friends
> who understand, and are committed to us for the long
> haul, and who plead with God on our behalf.
>
> DALE AND JUANITA RYAN

Addiction is isolating. Recovery can be too. But friendship is
powerful. The right friend—the right sort of friend—can be the
greatest ally and encouragement in recovery.

Jesus valued friendship. He called the disciples his friends. He
spoke of friendship in the upper room before his death: "Greater
love has no one than this: to lay down one's life for one's friends."[1]
Jesus wept for his friends—for Lazarus and for his sisters. He
prayed over him. He called to him. And in the end, he rescued him
from the bondage of death. For Lazarus, in his grave, friendship
with Jesus connected him to life.

Friendship forces us out of isolation. True friends pursue us,
and they keep coming back. True friends walk the nearly invisible line between accountability and open-armed acceptance. True
friends ask, "How are you doing with this?" True friends keep

confidences, not secrets. True friends wait for you to heal and are patient with the process. True friends support and encourage. A true friend is on your side and doesn't abandon you and loves you even when you're wrong. A true friend says the hard thing he or she needs to say with gentleness. A true friend forgives so that you are not "overwhelmed by excessive sorrow."[2] True friendship is life-giving, accepting, generous, constant, and faithful.

If you are reading this book because you have a close friend who's been in addiction and is now in recovery, you already know how hard it is to hang in there with them. But you care, you love them, and you're willing and ready to help. Maybe you're reading this book looking for affirmation that what you are doing is the right thing, or maybe you're reading because you have no idea what to do next. We may not know your friend's specific needs, but we *can* tell you what helped us.

Shame Leads to Disconnection

—H DAVE —

I've always been a people person. I had close friends growing up and in college. Things changed, however, when I started having frequent migraine headaches. At the time, migraines weren't considered a real problem by the general public. On top of that, I was in the transition from college relationships, which were 24/7, to a working life. So many of our good friends stayed in the same area, but not being at the same workplace or church or neighborhood was difficult. Instead of casually running into friends on campus, we had to intentionally make time for each other. This change, along with the increase in headaches, added another obstacle to keeping connected to relationships. The cure for migraines—pills—helped me function, but also made me undependable and loopy.

As dependency evolved into addiction, I became more and more distant in relationships with friends who held me accountable. I didn't feel rejected, but when we discussed our trials and troubles, the only tools we used were confession and accountability. We talked about pride and lust and issues like that—but we never broached the subject of addiction. Many of my closest friends were in ministry, or hoping to have ministry careers, and the belief among us was that real Christians confessed, repented, and just stopped sinning. Taking pills wasn't something I could just stop. I became distant, ill, distracted, ashamed, and manipulative. Friendships faded as I retreated. By the time we moved to Washington a decade later, I had already begun to replace my love for people with love of pills.

Washington was a thousand miles from the people who knew us best. As Dave's addiction took over, shame became a barrier to deep relationships. I was afraid that if people, even good friends back in California, knew about our problems, we would be judged and rejected. Dave going to seminary made asking for help so much harder. *What would we do if he was kicked out?*

Both Dave and I grew up in full-time ministry. Dave's dad was a pastor and mine, a missionary. There were expectations laid on kids like us, regardless of how our parents may have tried to shield us from them. Our behaviors were perceived as a direct reflection on our parents, which had made us both instinctively guarded about how much we shared with people. Since we chose to live near family and attend a seminary in our denomination, we were surrounded by people who knew our parents. The thought of shaming our parents mortified us.

Welcome Steps toward Vulnerability

A few years later, when we got involved in recovery support groups, we gradually allowed layers of self-protection to be peeled back. For the first time in our lives, we found people who did not know our families of origin, their current ministry positions, or the standards of measure to which each of us had always compared ourselves. No one cared about any of that. We were free to be ourselves and be known, flaws and all. Our friendships deepened as we drew closer to a community of other Christians in recovery and learned the joy of being loved and accepted without pretense—or reservation.

The first friends who came to us the day Dave lost his job at the Christian camp and conference center (our home as well) were our sponsors from our recovery group. I spoke nothing but pure anguish to my sponsor, Jane. I could barely breathe, I was submerged in despair and shame. We were suddenly penniless, homeless, ministry-less. I couldn't wrap my mind around Dave's confession of deceptions. After the goodness of the past seven months in recovery, the revelation staggered me. Jane listened, hugged, prayed, and assured me that though that moment of loss felt like death to both Dave and me, each of us could and would survive. It was so comforting to know that though we had lost so much that day, we hadn't lost these friends.

—⊣ DAVE ⊢—

My sponsor, a professional painter, was providentially on-site working that day at the camp. He embraced me, was sad for me, but wasn't as shocked by my deception and fall as I was.

I called our pastor, Jim, and told him that I had been asked to resign and to confess that I had been lying to him for months about still using pills. He responded with genuine disappointment and sadness. But he also shared his continued care and love for me by casually telling me that he hoped he would see me at church on Sunday and that I was welcome there. "We are a church full of messed up people," he said.

Friends who didn't have advice or a plan or experience with recovery responded with what they had: love and compassion, and even tangible help. Some of my camp staff committed to continued friendship and love for me and my family even though I had failed as their leader.

One of my employees, another dad like me, when I told him about my addiction that day, came alongside me and said, "Don't do anything stupid. You are loved." His words echoed in my head every time I had despairing thoughts of just ending my life. He knew what I would think and how deep the despair could be and gave me encouragement and hope in just two short sentences and an arm around my shoulder.

We don't have to have perfect answers to be compassionate. And I don't know how long our friends lingered over any thoughts of *What if I'm enabling?* Friends who helped financially gave directly to Deb, which was wise, of course, but they didn't scold me or make a big deal about not trusting me with money. They didn't cut me off and draw extreme boundary lines. They weren't enabling me to be an addict, they were enabling me to stay alive.

Compassion Nourishes Connection

Our lives drained of color. I was hollow and raw, and our four kids watched us anxiously for what would happen next. In the months that followed Dave's termination, we were grateful for people who were not afraid to be our friends. It wasn't just the loss of income and the house. The pain of being removed from ministry was acute. As was being forced to leave a hundred acres of woods and summer camp delight that had been a wonderland for our kids. I was grieving. We were all grieving.

Friends who came alongside me in this low and bitter season were brave. My emotions were raw, and our marriage was a wreck. Although I felt some relief being free from the bondage of secrets, I was so broken, and trying so hard to keep it together for our kids, that when I was in adult company, I couldn't restrain my hurt. I pushed for space to thrash about a bit—to wrestle with God like Jacob and try to scrape a blessing off the bottom of the well like Jeremiah. I remember quoting from the book of Ruth to my mother on the phone, "Call me Marah, for I am bitter." And I was serious.

In the first few days after Dave lost his job, his employees, friends in town, and families from our kids' school and community theater offered compassion. Sometimes through words, sometimes in action, sometimes through grocery money and just simple kindness. Even while they were reeling from Dave's fall, many of our neighbors/camp friends were so kind. Simply by their presence or a note of encouragement they gave a small piece of comfort. Every single kindness given to us told us that though we were being kicked out of our home and ministry community, we were not really total outcasts.

Allow Room for Struggle

There was nothing Dave or I could do in return for our friends for a very long time. Each of us was a gaping hole of need. We struggled to stay afloat. And the truth was, because none of our other friends had known anything about Dave's battle with addiction, it was all a bit of a shock to them as well.

Some friends walked beside us for a season, and other friendships grew stronger. Dave and I each needed our own friends, couple friends, and friends who were also in recovery. As Jesus was to Lazarus, they were our lifeline—our connection to life outside our pit.

There is power in encouragement. Everyone needs a cheerleader, a team. Someone in your corner, who knows you, who believes great things for you. A friend who is in your life just because they choose to be and who is committed to your success is a gift.

The friends we turned to in our moment of crisis are still some of our closest confidants today. In those days and the years since, they have encouraged our marriage and respected our individual recovery paths. Bolstered by this support and encouragement, we tested the waters with other friends. *Will they accept me and love me now that they know my real faults and secrets? Or will they reject me?* These vital friendships reconnected us to community.

Discern Your Role

For those who've made huge mistakes, there are and will be plenty of naysayers speaking into their lives, telling them they are a failure or that their husband or wife will never change. "Once an addict, always an addict" is a popular sentiment—and it's rather negative.

When your friend, or your close friend's spouse or child, is going through any hardship, discerning your place can be difficult. Recovery is a long-term process, so pray for discernment and the endurance to be an encouragement to them. Friends don't have to step in with all the answers. In fact, having all the answers is rarely helpful. But you can walk beside your friend and offer kindness in many different forms: listening, encouraging, and giving them grace and time.

Let's say for now that the friend in question is the one who has newly broken free from addiction. This friend has all kinds of needs—some they don't even know themselves. There will be times it's best not to step in until you're invited; other times they will need you to take the initiative. Either way, as you pray for wisdom to help your friend, at some point you can expect you'll be prompted to ask, "How can I support you in your recovery?" or if you're a friend of the spouse or parent, "How can I support you right now?"

When we're called on in a crisis as complicated as addiction, even by a close friend, sometimes our impulse is to run the other direction (unless we are rescuers by nature, and that can bring its own complications). Rather than asking whether we've been put in a needy person's path for a reason, we tell ourselves *we don't have time or energy for their drama.* Probably because we've been there before and quite possibly even with them.

Maybe we're committed to removing "toxic" relationships from our lives, and based on their track record, they don't make the cut. So we find ways to excuse ourselves from laying down our life for our friend. Our *best life* may require us to make some room for the inconvenience and tension of loving a friend through crisis. This is exactly what Jesus's followers did. Jesus warned them of the inconvenience they would face by following after him. "Take up your cross," Jesus said. "He who loves his life will lose it." They sold all their belongings and gave to the poor, they shared what they had, they opened their homes to each other, they attempted to practice a sort of love that would show the world they were his followers. And they suffered for it.

When a friend in addiction has finally reached the end of their rope and admits their need for help getting out of the pit they've dug for themselves, helping them may be a sacrifice for us. Laying down my life for my friend may look like listening, babysitting, driving them to work, taking them to rehab, to meetings, a counselor, church, the hospital. If you love them, you may enter the same difficulties with them a few times. Maybe because they've relapsed. Or maybe because no one else cares. You may even need to be an advocate for them so they can get the help they need.

We're a generation that rejects feeling guilty for saying no. But we have to learn to discern the difference between guilty feelings and the prompting of the Holy Spirit. God's plan for us is very likely to feel uncomfortable and inconvenient and may not spark instant joy. If we're not discerning, we can lose the opportunity God is setting in front of us to grow in our compassion and bring help and healing to a friend who is in our life for a reason. This distress, this moment in time, this year, these few years . . . when you look back over a lifetime, you will see that these are the hours, days, and years in which you loved your friends well.

Practice Grace

—┦[DAVE —

In their first ninety days clean, and through the first year of sobriety, people recovering from addiction need a lot of grace. As they work their way to physical, mental, social, and spiritual health, sometimes things will get worse before they get better. Friendship with someone in recovery from addiction can be a ride! Especially in the early stages while they are getting on their feet, it's hard not to take their mood changes or distancing personally. They may be struggling with emotional stagnation, bitterness, loneliness, and even physical illness. While the physical side effects should get better the longer they're clean, their struggle isn't over yet.

In recovery, I needed friends who wouldn't write me off, even if I failed. I was attempting to turn my whole life around. Your friendship can make a huge impact on a friend's recovery. You can offer kindness and a bit of dignity as they sort things out. You might be the only one who is *not* angry and accusing them at this moment!

Your friend is still human while they're in recovery. Leave them room to make normal, everyday, regular life mistakes, like being late for coffee. Give grace and the benefit of the doubt. Missing your coffee meet-up is not a reason to give up on someone who might be barely holding it together. Be forgiving of minor flaws and inconveniences. ("A man's insight gives him patience, and his virtue is to overlook an offense."[3])

This is just the beginning of their journey. Underneath their addiction, there are most likely some deep, deep wounds. The addiction may have been eclipsing some other critical issues. In addition, drugs and/or alcohol may have masked your friend's flaws. You might even have the thought go through your mind, "I liked you better when you were high." They can't fix everything all at once. If they're serious about recovery, they'll get to their less critical flaws eventually. But they will struggle under the weight of seeing everything they have to change in their lives exposed all at once. They may have unhealthy eating habits, control issues, depression—give them time. And remember, they're never going to be perfect—and neither are you.

Be careful not to heap shame on a friend who is struggling. Shame causes people to withdraw, hide, or cover their wounds with arrogance or aloofness. You can wait out the waves of hurt and not take their distancing personally. It stretches and grows our compassion and understanding. It's sacrificial love to step into their pain and hold them close when there is even a little bit of opportunity to do so—not to overwhelm them or push them away with too much attention, but just enough to say, "You are loved. I am here. I'll give you space, but I'm not going away."

People in recovery from substance addiction—and really any sort of trauma—have prickly days. If they're working with a counselor, going to a recovery group, or even just in the early days of abstinence, they may be irritable both physically and mentally, and their heads may not be in the conversation you're having. Don't take it personally. It might even be a year or more before they seem like themselves again. Physical withdrawal from drugs can be a very long process.

Create a Safe Space

When your friend is ready to talk, be a good listener. When you ask how they are doing, be genuine about wanting to hear whatever they have to tell you. When they are quiet and seem withdrawn, a comment like, "You seem deep in thought—I'm listening if you want to tell me about it" is more inviting than assuming your friend is upset with you or that you've done something that offended them. Their distancing may have nothing at all to do with you.

As you pursue an honest, open friendship with them, remember though that they may not share everything with you—we can't demand that they do. Author Christine Pohl writes, "A commitment to truthfulness does not mean that we disclose everything to everyone."[4] Shame is heavy, and while they may tell their sponsor or recovery group the worst of it, you may never hear everything they've done. Why? Because a sponsor or recovery group isn't likely to get into a conflict with them and use that knowledge against them. A friend or spouse, on the other hand, just might. If fear of rejection has caused them to hide in the past, when they tell you their faults, be trustworthy.

⸻

Protect and Support Their Recovery

Acknowledge how their recovery will change how you live—especially in your conversations and precautions. Be careful what you talk about with them and with others. Don't gossip about them, even though they've given you a *lot* to talk about. Being able to trust you can be so healing. If you're a friend to their face, be sure you're still their friend behind their back.

Be aware that 50 percent of opioid addicts got their last painkillers from a friend or relative.[5] "Most of us can't go to our grandmother's house and find cocaine, marijuana or methamphetamine, but we can find prescription painkillers," Gil Kerlikowske, former director of the White House Office of National Drug Control Policy, told the Associated Press back in 2012.[6] Your medicine cabinet can be as dangerous to your family and friends as a drug dealer. You can treat your friend with compassion and dignity while being careful to lock up your medications. Don't offer your leftover prescription to a friend in recovery, or to any friend for that matter. You just never know.

Your friend in recovery needs room to grow and become a new person. There may be places and people they have to avoid in order to stay sober. Consider what unhealthy habits you participated in together. Maybe your group of friends used to go out for a drink after work every Friday. Going out for a drink may be off-limits for a while and most likely forever for a friend in recovery from alcoholism. Find a new way to meet up together without alcohol.

In the first months and years of recovery, the potential for *causing your brother to stumble* becomes very real: "Do not destroy the work of God for the sake of food. All food is clean, but it is wrong for a person to eat anything that causes someone else to stumble."[7] You have no way to know what triggers a craving—they may not even know. A song, a smell, a place, a memory, a fight. Muscle memory is powerful. They are still breaking chains.

On that note, people make a lot of jokes about being high, thinking it's funny to tease after a dental visit or jokingly comment, "Score me some Vicodin." Don't coax a recovering friend into something they don't want to do or flaunt your freedom. You may unintentionally become the stumbling block that sends them into relapse.

—{| DAVE —

We'll look at this idea further in the next half of the book, but we tend to get hung up on the *means* of recovery. Some of us have opinions and convictions because of what worked for us, and others base theirs on what they've heard or observed from a distance. Your friend in recovery is alive and taking steps to heal. Encourage the positive steps they're taking as they recover, even if you think another program, system, or route is better. Tracey Helton Mitchell writes about this in the memoir of her addiction and recovery, *The Big Fix: Hope after Heroin*. She says that, even as a recovery professional now, she's had to resist the urge to advise based on what worked best for her. "These were not my wounds

I needed to heal," she writes. "There are many roads to the same destination."[8]

Hear and Receive Amends

No matter what recovery program your friend is in, at some point they may come to you with a confession or apology or what the 12 Steps call an "amends." It may not be what you expect. There may be a lot they don't/can't/aren't ready to remember. Take it as it comes and please don't dismiss their apologies with "No worries" or "It was nothing." If it's not a good time for you to give a thoughtful response, say, "I'd love to talk about this. Can we have coffee Thursday?" or something that lets them know you are taking it as seriously as they are. It's important to them, so show them it's important to you too.

If your friend really hurt you, it's okay to say they did, and even that it's hard for you to forgive them. A lot of people recovering from addiction struggle to believe anyone can really forgive them—they can't forgive themselves. They may come to you to make restitution for something they stole or bring money they owe you. They may start with something that seems trivial to you or isn't specific enough. It may be difficult to resist correcting them and saying, "What you should be apologizing for is _____." Remind them of your love. If you're not ready to forgive, simply say, "Thank you. Please give me some time to process this."

Don't be in a rush to have it done and fixed. That may cheapen their amends. How would you want to be forgiven when you've confessed something?

Be gentle with this. I wasn't able to acknowledge some of the worst things I'd done right away. Some were too much to face. It took me a couple of years to get through all the amends I needed to make. And like me, your friend may need to make amends several times before they get the worst things out.

Offer Genuine Forgiveness

We may need space and time to deal with how we've been hurt by our friend, but we also need to consider how drugs may have changed their behavior. Sometimes, we don't let a friend who has hurt us (and your friend who battled addiction has no doubt let you down in some way) back into our life until they ask for forgiveness. Even if they're in a recovery program, they're probably not going to ask forgiveness for everything they ever did to you all at once. Chances are, they don't remember all the things they did when they were high or seeking drugs. (This is true in a marriage as well.)

This is where love covering a multitude of sins comes into play in our Christian life. I don't think Jesus was talking about forgiving small slights, like when a friend forgot to send a thank-you note. He was talking about real offenses, like stabbing you in the back or stealing from you or lying to you. Forgiveness, in this context, can feel like dying to self, because it is. You're giving up your right to hold their offense against them. However, when we say the words of forgiveness without meaning them, without forgiving "from your heart" as Jesus said, our unforgiving spirit will eventually come out in the way we treat them.

Authors and recovery leaders Dale and Juanita Ryan write, "Forgiveness is not some kind of magical incantation that we can use to make our pain disappear. Forgiveness is an emotionally costly struggle. It is, however, an important struggle because it's part of the struggle to live in solidarity with God and his Kingdom. To struggle to forgive is the struggle to be like Jesus in whom we ourselves find forgiveness."[9]

Enable Success

—{ DAVE }—

If your friend has lost a job, a home, a spouse in their addiction and pursuit of recovery, they are likely to need some tangible, physical help. (Whether they ask it of you depends on their personality and, frankly, their desperation.) At any point along the way, there may be something you can do for them that will speak volumes about their worth. You don't have to be a recovery professional to practice compassion. John, my other sponsor, picked me up for recovery group meetings for a while. It was a simple act of friendship that helped me out both financially and with my recovery from addiction.

Some of us are so paranoid of "enabling" that any action we could take that doesn't seem punitive to an addict, even when they're working on recovery, seems like enabling. Here's what I mean: Say your friend takes pills and gets high. He drives, gets a ticket for driving under the influence, goes to jail, and gets his license taken away. When he gets out, he's committed to staying clean, and he gets a new job. He works faithfully for a few months, and then one day, he misses the bus that will get him to work on time and calls you in desperation for a ride. Believe it or not, in situations just like this, I will hear parents and friends of addicts in recovery say, "I'm not giving him a ride. That's just a consequence of his addiction." Yes. Not having a car to get to work is a consequence of addiction, but that doesn't release us from kindness when it is in our power to be kind. Losing a job over a non-addiction-related issue can set them back in their recovery or embitter them toward you.

Give expecting nothing in return. They may be so focused on survival that they don't show their gratitude right away. When we give freely and from the heart, we are putting kindness into action and practicing compassion. No, our compassion won't be a magical fix, but it is balm on a wound that will help it heal.

There are so many simple ways to help people in crisis—kindnesses that will strengthen their spirit. If you invite them to coffee or out to eat, just say "my treat" and don't make a big deal about it. It's often hard for people to accept generosity, but we can give in a way that doesn't draw attention to our friend's situation.

Sometimes we get so caught up in our doing good that we forget to leave our friend some dignity.

You don't have to be your friend's probation officer, judge, or mom. Sure, friends hold each other accountable. But you have to earn the right to hear the worst. Accountability may evolve over time and as you prove to them you're not going to slam the door when they tell you the truth. You can ask, "Do you want me to ask how you're doing? How often?" And then when they say, "I blew it. I took Ed's leftover pills," we can encourage honesty with a gentle response like, "So what are you going to do about it?" which opens the door to conversation without judgment.

In Galatians 6:1, the apostle Paul writes, "Brothers and sisters, if someone is caught in a sin, you who live by the Spirit should restore that person *gently*. But watch yourselves, or you also may be tempted" (emphasis added). Gentleness isn't being soft on failures. It's about remembering that the end goal is restoration.

Take time to communicate kindly. Recovery brings pain to the surface. Sometimes they'll be ready to talk more about it; sometimes they will just want to eat pizza and watch a movie with you. Your time together doesn't always have to be about their struggle— you can have fun together, giving them a gift of normalcy.

Celebrate Successes

If your friend has just committed to getting clean, just came out of rehab, or has decided to finally get help, be excited with them. But also recognize that recovery is a process, not a onetime event. Breaking free from the bondage of addiction that enshrouded their life may be a one-day-at-a-time, hand-over-hand climb out of a deep pit. They will need friends, good ones, who cheer them on. When you look back someday and see how far they've come, how long they've been free, it's cause to celebrate. When they say, "I'm thirty days clean," and you know it's a long time for them, celebrate it. With as little as "That's awesome" to as big as "Let's go out for pie." Those thirty days have been a lifetime to your friend. Celebrate the milestones.

Friends encourage us to keep going. They forgive and gradually extend trust as they embrace grace and forgiveness. It takes years for people who were caught in addiction to rebuild trust, even with—especially with—the people closest to them. As each year passes, hope builds. Yes, stay vigilant, but also celebrate. The sidelines are full of critics, and they may even seek to tear down your friend, who will face doubters, haters, and demons of discouragement.

Ask for Grace for Yourself

You are going to make mistakes as you walk beside your friend in recovery. But as you make allowance for each other's faults and offer love that covers a multitude of sins,[10] you will see your friend heal and grow, and soon you'll have a friendship of equals, an iron-sharpens-iron relationship. Remember to let your friend grow. They won't always be struggling through recovery like they are in the first weeks, months, and even years of the process. Treat your friend in recovery like a friend who also has something to offer—it doesn't have to be a one-sided relationship. They aren't defined completely by their addiction.

As you forgive and gradually extend trust and as they embrace grace and forgiveness, you will see proof of change in their life. As your friend becomes more healthy and faces difficult relationships or things they've been avoiding, you might even begin to notice your own imperfections.

——— ⫯ ———

Give Grace to Their Family

A whole family is affected when one of them is in addiction. If they've got young kids, the children may not be on their best behavior right now. A parent in addiction is a kind of trauma for a child long before the parent recognizes it.[11] Kids whose homes have been rocked by addiction and its side effects are going to struggle. Everyone in the family, not just the one in recovery, needs compassion and grace. Walking through recovery with a family includes loving their kids, who will need healing as well. Grace is critical for breaking the cycle of addiction that runs through families.

Not every good Christian who goes through a crisis responds immediately and quietly with Job's words: "The LORD gave, and the LORD has taken away"[12]—if they do, wait a few months. (Shock can be an excellent buffer.) Everyone wears their grief differently. Some of us jump straight through the stages of grief to anger. I know I did! Loving and caring for a friend in crisis may look a lot more like trying to wash a wild cat. We may have to step back a bit and let them thrash about. Our losses brought grieving over the life we thought we'd have, over poverty, and over the hard changes for our children.

Job's friends sat with him for seven days before speaking.[13] When they finally opened their mouths to speak, so much of what they said to him seems accurate and totally in line with what the rest of the Bible says about suffering, God, and repentance. But when God speaks out of the whirlwind, his response is not "Spot on, guys! Way to be theologically correct!" No, he wants them to be clear on his power and prerogative to do what he wants, to heal how he wants to heal. We don't always have the answers. Sometimes our role as a friend is just to listen and wait for God to speak.

Transparency Takes Time

While Dave was opening up to friends and mending relationships, I was too. One of the hardest things about Dave's addiction was, not only was he my husband, he was also my best friend. When trust is broken so badly in marriage, it leaves you feeling untethered and insecure. Trusting anyone after betrayal takes healing and time. It's taken me a long time to allow more than just a couple of friends in closer. Fear of rejection or gossip or condemnation can override our certainty of our friend's love and faithfulness. Sometimes it's because our fears have been proven right.

The number one priority in our relationship as husband and wife, but also as friends with each other, was to reestablish honesty. Dave did this with Jim and the other friends he'd deceived as well. I did it with my close friends. I *had* to tell them once it was exposed. I couldn't wait for that barrier to come down like it was the Berlin wall. I wanted out of secrecy and lies so badly; they were a prison keeping me not only distant from friends but also from living fully. I had felt used, deceived, and helpless to fix any of it. Honesty takes time, requires time to prove itself. You can't just know overnight that someone has been honest with you. You look back over years and seasons to see the pattern of truth. Truth is the mortar that rebuilds your demolished relationship brick by brick.

With friends who've been through trauma, try to walk the line between giving space and expecting too much social interaction from them. They may need time to revive family relationships and may feel pressure to divide time between friends and family. If they have kids, they may want to make up for hours, days, and years lost. Give them space for recovery friends too. None of us are perfect friends, but open and gentle communication can help restore not only the relationship but our friend in recovery as well.

Respect Their Marriage

As the spouse of a person in recovery, I needed friends who respected my decision to stay with Dave. It's an easy out to take sides, but if you are pro-marriage and your friend is not being abused, don't be the one who tells them to leave. Encourage them to go to counseling. Love and listen to your friend. But is it really your place to tell them to get a divorce? Especially if you've only ever heard one side of the story. If your friend and their spouse are working things out, who are you to say they shouldn't?

I had a friend who could not get past Dave's addiction or their distrust or disappointment in him. This sort of underlying tension strains a friendship. It's like being friends with someone who doesn't really accept you. You always feel judged, or like there's something they're not telling you—or worse, they do tell you. Like the friend who once said to me that she could never stay with a man who had done to her what Dave did to me. Her disdain was palpable. After that, I never could be authentic with her. I felt like she didn't respect my decision to stay. If you can't be supportive of your friend's marriage, ask yourself why. It could be that you are wrestling with forgiving someone yourself.

Our friends' acceptance, love, and pursuit of us are powerful healers. Some of the most helpful things were simple ones, like just going for a walk together. I walked with a friend a few times a week for that entire first year after we left the camp. It was cathartic. I had so much anger, confusion, hurt—walking helped me release it.

In the recovery process, I needed friends who were kind to my husband, who didn't gauge our relationship by the amount of time I could spend with them, and who didn't pressure me into doing expensive things, knowing money was tight. I needed friends who also didn't let too much time pass before checking in again, knowing my tendency to isolate when I'm discouraged. They were and still are my cheerleaders. Their encouragement and pursuit of me have been transforming. In addition, they are Dave's cheerleaders too. My closest friends have inspired me to love my husband more, to be excited for his successes, to find joy in his recovery journey and deeper walk with God. They respect the time I have with Dave and our kids and encourage that as well.

Over time, and in honesty, our friendships with others have grown. Dave is now associate pastor and close friend to Jim, who has been our pastor for fourteen years, and Jane, who was once my sponsor, is still one of my dearest friends. Their encouragement and support have been life—and marriage—preserving. Their acceptance and love have been healing. Not only in our friendships, but for our marriage and family and faith. To know without a doubt that you are loved for who you are, flaws and all? There is a beautiful phrase in Scripture: "Make allowance for each other's faults."[14] Our friends have certainly made allowance for ours. Because of the acceptance and love of these friends, we opened up to other friends who not only have loved me but have loved Dave and our kids as well. Their love and support have encouraged our growth.

Offer Friendship in Community

—⊣ DAVE —

One of the goals of long-term addiction recovery programs is to break ties with bad relationships, specifically the crowd you hung out with, the people with whom you got high. Why? Because these relationships have a powerful effect on you, on your choices, and on staying clean. People in recovery from addiction often need new friends. Whether they've burned bridges, or their old friends were the ones who joined or supplied their addiction, they need to rebuild community—or have community rebuilt around them. You would be amazed how powerful a simple welcome and kindness can be. Connect them to a caring community. Invite them into your circle of friends. It's an incredible opportunity to offer the welcome at the heart of Christian hospitality.

In her fantastic book *Making Room*, Christine Pohl says that one of the most beautiful things about being part of a community is that no one person has to bear the weight of compassion alone. There are occasions when, though our hearts are full of love and ready to serve, we have to consider our own family and their safety. We have to be wise about the people already in our care. We may not be free to offer a friend a place to live, but we can give them rides or help with groceries. We can pool resources with a few other friends or through our church to find them a safe place to live.

Jesus ministered to people through his friendship with them. He healed their wounds and introduced them to a family who would care for them. As a church, if we're not engaged in healing the wounds in our community, what are we here for? If connection to a caring community of friends is so transforming, imagine what the church can do together. We have the opportunity to address the deep ache and longing beneath the surface of the opioid epidemic crisis in our country, because connection is at the heart of who we are supposed to be—a community connected to each other by love for God and love for our neighbor.

six

The Mission of the Church

> Church is too often a place of pretense and therefore a place without hope. When brokenness is disdained, where the real story is never told, the power of God is not felt. Where brokenness is invited and received with grace, the gospel comes alive with hope.
>
> LARRY CRABB

According to Pew Research, half of all Americans know someone struggling with drug dependence or addiction.[1] The 2016 National Survey of Drug Use and Health says 1.7 million people aged twelve or older currently struggle with prescription painkiller addiction.[2] The search for solutions has become a national conversation, and as followers of a God who heals, we have the opportunity to join in with compassion, ready to do the difficult work of restoration. Because of the healing work of Jesus Christ, the church as his ministers can offer grace, physical help, spiritual guidance, and even healing.

Unfortunately, the church has quite a reputation for being the last place on earth you'd want to go to share a struggle like opioid addiction. Some of us have learned this through painful experience. Dietrich Bonhoeffer's description of the church three quarters of a century ago applies still today: "The pious fellowship permits no one to be a sinner. So everybody must conceal his sin from himself and from the fellowship. We dare not be sinners. Many Christians are unthinkably horrified when a real sinner is suddenly discovered among the righteous. So we remain alone with our sin, living in lies and hypocrisy."[3]

We're really good at cleaning ourselves up for Sunday. We're supposed to be victorious and full of joy. We've got an image to uphold. *We're running a race. Taking the time to stop and help you clean your wounds will hold me up from my goal!*

There's already so much about church that feels like an exclusive club: members, membership meetings, events, groups, classes, "dues," special songs, rituals, greetings, code words. For those who've grown up in church, all of this is practically second nature. We dress up, stop our arguments before we open the car doors, "greet the brethren" with smiles and handshakes, then afterward we scoot out the door to get to the next thing: family dinner, the football game on TV, a soccer match. I tried to fit into the "club" all my life, until I was so broken, I couldn't keep up the show.

But when the church is a gathering of broken people who are truly seeking the God who heals, authenticity, compassion, and welcome become a natural part of the personality of the congregation. We need to be a church culture that stops to minister to the wounded. That allows space for being wounded and time to heal.

For Dave and me, *the church was both the biggest barrier to recovery from addiction and our best means to it.* The irony of our particular brand of faith upbringing is that so many believe the grip of addiction is released at the moment of salvation . . . and yet they do not believe in faith healing. We were looking for that one-time, drop-your-burden-at-the-cross, give-it-to-Jesus, life-transforming moment. "Uncle Fred came to Jesus and he never drank a drop of liquor again." Or "We sent Tommy away hooked on drugs and he came back to us all fixed as a new creation."

Sometimes it happens. Sometimes people do have a crisis moment and a change of heart and life. I don't want to minimize that. I do believe addiction can be completely healed in a moment, but if this is our normal view of addiction, we leave out recovery, relapse, and anyone who becomes addicted *while* he is a Christian. If they want to stay "in fellowship," they resort to hiding their problem. And hiding only makes the problem worse.

In *The Ragamuffin Gospel*, Brennan Manning writes:

> Often hobbling through our church doors on Sunday morning comes grace on crutches—sinners still unable to throw away their false supports and stand upright in the freedom of the children of God. Yet, their mere presence in the church on Sunday morning is a flickering candle representing a desire to maintain contact with God. To douse the flame is to plunge them into a world of spiritual darkness. There is a myth flourishing in the church today that has caused incalculable harm—once converted, fully converted. . . . Discipleship will be an untarnished success story; life will be an unbroken upward spiral toward holiness.[4]

Problems Good People Don't Have

Our story, though it may look a little different on the outside, is just one of the stories of millions of people whose lives have been buried in some way by addiction. But for a long time, especially at the beginning of Dave's struggle with pills, I thought our story was different because *we had Jesus*. We believed all the right things. We went to church twice on Sunday and in the middle of the week. We were dedicated to full-time ministry. Dave was in seminary. He did not become addicted through a vice he'd been taught to avoid. He wasn't "drawn away and enticed."[5] He was going to doctors for help with migraine headaches. Dave's prescription painkiller addiction shattered my worldview in a way no other addiction could. Because when a doctor hands you a prescription for chronic and debilitating pain, it's not an obvious pitfall, and it's a little trickier to "just say no." Especially when refusing drugs means living with pain.

Addiction isolated us. For years I thought we had a shameful problem decent people don't have, certainly not Christians. Alone, I reasoned through the spectrum of theological beliefs about Dave's addiction: His addiction to pills was a sin to confess, so if he just genuinely repented, he'd be rid of it. Or it was a besetting sin and he needed more accountability to keep him on track. Or it meant he'd fallen away from the faith . . . or that he couldn't actually be a real Christian. Because according to 1 John 3:6, "No one who lives in him keeps on sinning. No one who continues to sin has either seen him or known him." I fully believed in what Manning called the "upward spiral toward holiness." The college Dave and I went to called it "an upward trajectory." If the graph of your life had too many dips or a slide? Well, you probably weren't "saved" to begin with.

I confronted Dave so many times about this, questioned his beliefs, his commitment to Jesus. He assured me over and over that he believed all the right things, that there was a moment in time when he had turned his life over to Jesus, but he could not seem to conquer his need for pills. I landed for a while on Romans 7 where Paul says, "I do not understand what I do. For what I want to do I do not do, but what I hate I do. . . . For I have the desire to do what is good, but I cannot carry it out. For I do not do the good I want to do, but the evil I do not want to do—this I keep on doing." And what if addiction was an affliction? Like Paul's thorn in the flesh?

When I first discovered Dave's addiction, I believed it was a sin and that genuine repentance would eventually set him on the right path. When that failed, I went to our pastor about Dave's reckless spending and need for accountability. But Dave lapsed back into addiction and hiding, unknown to the pastor or me. When I discovered his relapse and went to our pastor and his wife again for help, this time they recognized the problem was something more than what continued confrontation, repentance, and forgiveness could mend. They encouraged physical intervention, not just spiritual, and helped us get Dave into a three-week state hospital rehab program.

Rehab was a start, but I didn't realize the mental and physical grip of addiction could remain so strong beyond getting clean. The sufficiency of Scripture for all things was so embedded in my mind, I felt like we were apostates when Dave went to AA meetings. Taking our problems to someone outside the church seemed like a betrayal of my faith, like I was dragging the name of Jesus through the mud by letting "the world" in on our shame.

Going to the Pastor

—┥ DAVE ┝—

A pastor is often the first point of contact for a Christian who is struggling with addiction. But it's almost never the person struggling with addiction himself or herself, rather a family member—a parent, a spouse—who comes to me seeking help first. A pastor's response to the loved one depends on his experience, his training, his theology of healing, his view of counseling, his relationship to the one who is addicted, his experience with those struggling with addiction, and a myriad of other factors. Which means, you won't get the same response from every pastor.

In his book *The Recovery-Minded Church*, Jonathan Benz says, "Seminaries provide limited training, if any, in addiction counseling and recovery. Yet many people struggling with addiction are looking to the church for answers."[6] A pastor now myself, even with my own experience with addiction and recovery, it's important for me to recognize where my expertise and abilities end, and where I need to refer out for help.

But if you have a heart for people in crisis, even if you're not equipped with specific training but are a good listener, you can still

Jonathan Benz proposes pastors keep a referral list on hand, and he includes them in his book *The Recovery-Minded Church*:
- Twelve-step groups with personal contacts for each of these groups
- Clergy and churches in your area with thriving support-group ministries and recovery expertise (if your church does not have these)
- Physicians and psychiatrists with addiction and dual-diagnosis specialties
- Hospital facilities and detox centers providing services to alcoholics and addicts
- Outpatient and inpatient treatment programs with good reputations
- Halfway houses or other follow-up programs for addicts coming out of treatment programs
- Mental health professionals with addiction expertise, as well as therapists trained in stress management
- Treatment programs for homeless addicts, such as the Salvation Army[7]

be a critical part of their recovery as a representative of a loving, compassionate God. And the pastor's response could keep the person struggling with addiction connected to the church community, particularly if that community is willing to be a part of restoration.

After my first relapse post-rehab, when I was leading a Christian ministry, Deb and I went to my supervisor to tell him. He asked simply, "Do you have victory?" When I told him I thought I had, he said he didn't want to hear about my addiction again. Although my supervisor was not my pastor, because it was a Christian ministry, it felt like a strange mix of confessing to your pastor and admitting to your boss.

Two years later, after a few more relapses, Deb went to see our new pastor. He recognized our need for something more than he was equipped to give and referred us to a local counselor. Eventually, we ended up going to a recovery ministry at another church in another denomination. Our pastor's response spoke volumes to me: *Regardless of whether we have a program to help you in our church, you are welcome here and you are loved.*

Our pastor understood that spiritual oppression could be involved in addiction, which was something we had not considered. Addressing the spiritual side of addiction definitely played a part in my recovery process, even though I relapsed again. Jim kept praying for me and meeting with me, but he also encouraged me to keep seeking other professional help with addiction. He didn't lean solely on casting out spirits as a cure.

After another major relapse, I went to a weekend rehab and came out with a Suboxone treatment plan (we've written more about this in chap. 11), which included seeing a psychiatrist. In the past, we would have rejected psychiatric treatment as unbiblical, but it was our last resort. Our pastor's support of our search for healing kept us in the church and connected by a string to a community where, unknown to any of us, we would eventually land when we fell.

‡

The Barrier of Tribalism

It's pretty much heresy in some denominations to say that it took more than obedience to Scripture or more than a moment of supernatural transformation to rescue Dave from addiction and change our lives. But our unlimited God can and does work through complex and varied means to heal us.

The church gets hung up on words, just like our culture does. We buy into *either/or*: *This method is the right one, that one is wrong.* We are forever trying to set up universal truths, principles, and rules. We're compelled to have *one right answer*. And our tribalism creates a huge barrier for people who need healing from addiction.

Call it sectarianism, call it tradition, perception, or allegiance, it doesn't just mark the church, as we'll see in subsequent chapters. It marks everyone in any sector who has interest—even feigned interest—in the addiction business, current crisis or not. We not only have tribes based on the nature of addiction, we have tribes based on which programs and philosophies and theologies and treatments work.

But the *one best solution* idea is a myth. Neither addiction nor recovery is a one size fits all. How could it be? Addiction involves heart, soul, mind, and body, and each of us is created differently.

What if we stopped leaning on our church's brand of tribalism, whether it's our rejection of medicine and science and their role in getting people out of addiction, or our prejudice against psychology, our view of the opioid crisis through a political lens, or even our need to build a better program than the church across town? It's wonderful that your church has Celebrate Recovery! But what do you accomplish when you criticize the effectiveness of the church down the street that holds space for AA meetings? Methadone will keep your son off heroin! Yes, for many who wish to get off drugs, it's been the only way they could hold down a job. But don't discount the effectiveness and possibility of long-term behavioral counseling because you believe psychology is bunk. Your parishioner got clean and stayed clean through being remanded to a work ranch? That's fantastic! But that doesn't mean the new outpatient program at the community center won't work. The current opioid crisis compels us to work together to heal our country's gaping wound. We merely create confusion for addicts and their families when we're so divided over the means of recovery.

We confuse *Jesus is the only way for salvation* with the idea that *Jesus is the only way for anything good in our lives.* And so, some church people say recovery from addiction can *only* be found in Jesus. This is the equivalent of saying only God can heal pneumonia. Penicillin is a pretty good healer. The point of the church's ministry to people trapped in addiction is not that *Jesus is the only way out of your addiction.* It might be true for some people, but plenty of people get and stay sober apart from God.

It's important to remember that the church is not offering "the only way" out of addiction. Neither is Hazelden, or Schick Shadel, or boot camp, or the methadone clinic, or AA. What we have to offer is the compassionate love of a God who embraces our broken pieces, who welcomes us with open arms, who delights in transformation and restoration, and for this reason every one of us—even the most messed-up addict—has hope.

The Ministry of Recovery

In their book *Bridges to Grace*, Liz Swanson and Teresa McBean write, "A church that understands the power of grace and refrains from condemnation can, through a ministry of recovery, offer people the gift of hope and become a place where vision is renewed and people are healed."[8] Underneath addiction are heartaches that entice people into numbing their pain—their shame, their disillusionment—with drugs. People in crisis who are experiencing deep soul grief are starving for compassion and love. I know I was, and so was Dave.

Is the church still in the business of ministering healing to people? If we change our vision to see people, rather than just their problems, we have the opportunity to offer hope in this opioid crisis. It's not just about them giving their life to Jesus, it's about freeing them from the trappings of death.

At Lazarus's tomb, Jesus did not ask the gathered crowd to raise the dead. He asked them to do the dirty job of unwrapping a man who'd been dead and buried for days. Jesus, the One who started this church, ate with, walked with, and healed broken people the religious leaders of his day wanted nothing to do with. Somewhere after the first-century church, we developed a polished-up, clean-church culture that doesn't at all resemble the messy, grateful crowd gathered around Jesus. We leave the dirty work for our nonprofits.

What if, as Spurgeon says, it's our duty as bystanders to help free people we know from the figurative graveclothes that threaten to keep them in bondage? We can have the best sermons in town, but if our response to those who've broken free from addiction is only to celebrate victory and not walk with them through the damage in the wake of their addiction, we've lost the opportunity to be a part of the miracle of restoration.

The Ministry of Welcome

"Americans seek the quick fix for spiritual as well as physical pain," writes Kathleen Norris. "That conversion is a lifelong process is the last thing we want to hear."[9] The quick fix is so much a part of our culture, we don't even recognize it anymore. In the Church, we call it "victory."

Changing our vision means resisting the quick fix. When we are preoccupied with people being fixed, or *claiming victory* over their chemical addiction, we allow no room for process. Which means when they do stumble, they feel like they can't go back to church. But if we treat recovery like a progressive healing, just as sanctification is, we leave the door open for people to come back when they fail because we haven't set the standard at perfection.

The life-giving grace of our humanity is that we're in this struggle together. Not one of us has arrived. We are a community of broken people. Because of this, we can rejoice with people who've made progress *and* make space for people who are struggling. "Grace applauds those who succeed, but it also claps for those who just keep showing up week after week," Liz Swanson and Teresa McBean point out in their book *Bridges to Grace*.[10] If we honor the process rather than condemn it for not being fast enough or get too focused on results, people will be more honest about their struggles and failures. This is more Christlike than forcing them to put on a face of positivity and victory when they're in need of loving, compassionate community.

We need to convert our churches to sanctuaries for the broken, where *the least of these* feels welcome. "The environment we create matters more than the programs we offer."[11] No matter what size our church is, we can have effective, fruitful ministry just by our welcome.

Communicating love starts at the door of the church. How we greet people lets them know whether our church is a place of hope for healing. In the worst of Dave's addiction days, I was so grateful when I pulled up to church late and the deacon opened the door to me with a smile. "You're just in time," he would say. Our church let me lurk in the back row. I scooted in and out as quickly as possible to avoid conversations, but I kept coming back.

A grace-filled environment is constructed from the front of the church. If the pastor refers to people with problems as "other" or uses *us/them* terminology, he leaves out the people in his pews who are struggling. If we are going to minister to the deepest needs in our communities, we need to assume the hurting people are right there among us. How we talk unintentionally isolates hurting people who are already in our congregation and newcomers seeking help.

The Ministry of Noticing

When we are going through struggles that we believe decent and good people, especially church people, don't have, our feelings of worthlessness and fears of being exposed can prompt us to put up walls. Some of us cover our pain in a flurry of social activities, and some of us isolate. Some have a need to feel important somewhere, to know their existence outside their current crisis means something.

We withdrew from a lot of social activity when Dave was let go from his position leading a ministry, but I also got involved in volunteering more outside the church. It helped me feel like I had worth somewhere when I felt worthless in the church—not because of how I was treated, but because of the side effects and fallout of addiction.

Remember, in the recovery process, addicts and their families are working through some deep hurt. The drugs or drink they were using may have numbed them to memories of childhood abuse, of devastating loss, of things they can't forgive themselves for. In recovery, they're facing demons one by one. Recovery knocks the crutch away and forces them to examine areas of their life they've avoided. It's important to remember, too, that people who have addiction issues or substance abuse disorder may have mental health issues that need to be addressed.[12] As they progress in their recovery, and the underlying reasons for their addiction come out, they'll begin to deal with them. If things get worse, be prepared to encourage them to see a counselor and point them to community resources you may not have in your church.

Sometimes those who've struggled with trauma like addiction or living with a recovering addict have a hard time connecting or reconnecting to community. We aren't always the greatest friends at first, we may not be the life of the party anymore, and we may not enjoy the small talk that sparks regular relationships. This is the beautiful place of ministry for those of us who are naturally inclined toward the edges of a room. The ones who can't bear to be in the center of everything are in a strategic location for ministry to the people who stay on the fringes. We just have to lift up our heads and notice them.

The Ministry of Listening

For many years, I took refuge from church expectations in the excuses afforded by little ones—someone was always sick, someone needed to get home for a nap. I struggled to connect with other church women. In part because shame had me on a path toward isolation, and in part because, sisters and brothers, we are not good listeners and we are not good noticers and we try way too hard to have the right answers. How many times do we talk over, misinterpret, give a verse along with a "Well, you know what you should do," as though there was a trick the discloser of pain didn't know and it's so easy *if they just do this.* "Why don't you just" rolls so easily off our tongues. If the church is going to be effective in the restoration mission in front of us, we have to accept broken people where they are—and where they are can make us really uncomfortable. Part of compassion is listening. People in crisis aren't necessarily looking for answers . . . yet.

At the end of eighteen months of counseling, my counselor asked me what I thought had been the most beneficial part of our time together. My response did not surprise her: listening. I was able to talk to her about all the things I couldn't talk about anywhere else. She was an exceptionally good listener. She knew exactly when to ask questions and when to let me just talk it out. Of course she did! She was trained to listen professionally.

Listening well might be the easiest way to begin ministering to hurting people in our church and community. The healing power of being heard is woefully underestimated. Bonhoeffer says, "Just as love to God begins with listening to His Word, so the beginning of love for the brethren is learning to listen to them."[13]

We can learn and apply simple techniques from counselors, and from the guidelines support groups implement to ensure they are a safe space to share. Talking over a hurting person, putting words in their mouth, and giving instant advice are not good listening habits.

Fellow quiet people who feel like your quietness is keeping you from big ministry, you can have a very powerful role in healing and recovery. Why? Because you are content to listen. But that doesn't let the rest of us off the hook. We all need to work harder at listening to each other. "Everyone," says James, "should be quick to listen, slow to speak."[14] Listening is the very least we can do to help, but it also just might be the most.

When our approach to church is that we are seeking personal fulfillment, we are not going to be very interested in the messy sort of care people in crisis may need. We lose patience with others' needs. But if we're just there for ourselves, for "being fed," we're missing the point of the church as a community. Pastor and radio host Doug Bursch describes our present-day church preferences in *The Community of God: A Theology of the Church from a Reluctant Pastor.* He writes about the need to approach the church to serve others, rather than just for personal growth:

> You may be reluctant to go to the one Bible study your church offers if only five men regularly attend and one of those men struggles with a rather severe addiction issue that often leads to him spending a large part of the study talking about his struggles. If you are a woman looking for a Bible study to escape the pressures of work, you might be somewhat reluctant to attend a women's group that only has six women and one of those women has just survived a rather messy divorce and spends a large portion of the prayer request time talking in a somewhat bitter way about her ex-husband. If you believe small groups are primarily for personal growth, you probably will not choose to go to any of these groups.
>
> Conversely, if you believe faith has just as much to do with the needs of the body as with personal growth, you will invest in spiritual activities that may be relationally awkward. You will faithfully attend that Bible study with your brother in Christ who struggles with addiction and you will learn how to love and to support him in the process. You will commit to the women's group and listen intently to the hurting heart of that recently divorced woman. In the process, you will help her learn how to forgive and to love as Christ loves.[15]

There was a time when we were the needy church attendees. I remember one time in particular when I was testing the waters of safety in a women's Bible study. Some women were too un-comfortable to allow more than a few minutes of sharing before interjecting their thoughts and opinions on what I needed to do. I was so raw at the time, I didn't have the presence of mind to speak up and say, *I know all of that. I read the Bible every day. I pray without ceasing. What I need is for someone to listen, just for a moment, to my deepest hurt. I need a safe place to share what's happening in my life.*

At the time, I ended up finding the listeners I needed outside my church. I'm sure a lot of us do. But it doesn't have to be that way if we see our church community as a place to minister to each other with compassion, rather than only a place to get what we need for ourselves.

The Ministry of Restoring Dignity

One of the most compassionate things we can do for people is approach them with dignity and work to restore their dignity. Sky Jethani writes about dignity in his book *Immeasurable: Reflections on the Soul of Ministry in the Age of Church, Inc.*:

> Our calling as pastors is to rehabilitate, to give people back the dignity the world has taken away. That happens when we carry the presence of God into every room we enter and into every life we encounter, and there announce the good news that they are created in the image of God and are inherently worthy of love, and that God has revealed the extent of His love for them through Jesus' life, death, resurrection, and ascension. This work of restoring dignity is always incarnate; it cannot be accomplished merely through systems, structures, or programs. Rehabilitation requires the present and mysterious mingling of humanity and divinity.[16]

But restoring dignity isn't just the work of the pastor. At the heart of dignity is treating others the way we would want to be treated. We can reach out and treat each other as fellow bearers of the image of God. The way we access the compassion in ourselves to do this work is by the old tried-and-true practice of putting ourselves in their shoes. But this is nearly impossible when we have an *us/them* mind-set. We simply can't picture ourselves, no matter how hard we try, in their place. "I would never . . ." is a dignity killer. I think this is why it's so important for us who have been in their place to step up. To tell our stories and lead our churches in this mission of compassion. "And such were some of you" is a call to remember to practice grace that doesn't just give lip service to "there but for the grace of God go I."[17]

We restore people's dignity by not making them jump through hoops to get help. Christians have a tendency these days to make a show of our compassion. Often, at nonprofit ministries, those being ministered to are asked to consent to using their photo in newsletters and fund-raising communications. This is because studies show that we give more when we see real faces of need. But consider what it does to a person's dignity when they become a poster child for poverty and addiction. Public displays of generosity toward men, women, and children who are in need of help strip them of dignity and remind them of their indebtedness. We've strayed far from the command to *give in secret* and *not let your left hand know what your right hand is doing.*[18] We don't have to strip people of their dignity in order to help them. It's not the way God intended it to be.

For us, recovery was not only *about* Dave getting out of addiction but also restoring our life. For a time, though we weren't living on the streets, we were considered "categorically needy" and homeless by the state of Washington. We were two college grads, former teachers, and ministry leaders in desperate need and unable to provide for their children because of the consequences of Dave's addiction. Asking anyone for help was humbling, but asking the church was hardest of all. When we were in our pit because of Dave's choices, I did not feel deserving. And "deserving" is how we tend to judge who gets help.

In addition, a struggling family may step out of church because of the cost of attending: books for Bible studies, youth activities, expensive camps, women's retreats, and so on. I remember dreading girls' night out at church and the pressure of home shopping parties—as well as being grateful for Sunday potlucks because for once, there would be plenty of wonderful food for our kids to eat. I was thankful when the table was so full of food that my lack of contribution wasn't even noticed.

One of the most humbling things I dealt with in the years we struggled most financially was how limiting not having money to fill my gas tank was. Some weeks, I had to choose between going to Celebrate Recovery and going to church simply because I couldn't afford the gas to do both. I even kept the kids home from school a few times (our temporary house was not on the bus route for their school) so that a tank of gas would stretch further.

The Ministry of Practical Help

—H DAVE—

Sometimes, we have unreasonable expectations of the people we help. Too many times, we get hung up on things we can't control. We want people to be more grateful than they are. Or we fear that after we've helped them, they'll just move on to another church. Or we think helping them is enabling them to continue in bad behavior. Working with people overcoming addiction is hard, but by working together across churches and partnering with community resources, we can restore people and families who've been devastated by addiction.

A block down the road from our church, the local food bank offers multiple services on-site through various community partners. Like most nonprofit community resource centers, every service they provide has a waiting list, from housing to firewood. If you have the resources as a church body to help someone in your congregation who is struggling, that means one less person or family who has to depend on the strained resources of the broader community. Churches can help with gas cards, transportation, utilities, medical needs, childcare costs, rent, and so much more, leaving more community resources for those who have no church family to care for them. (We've listed more practical ideas at the back of the book as well.)

Your church may not have the resources for a full recovery program now or ever, but when whatever you can offer is fueled by your love for God and the compassion of Jesus Christ, that love can transform people's lives right in our own communities. Dale Ryan, one of the foremost leaders in Christian recovery, says, "A congregation that does grace rather than shame in all of its affairs is likely to be profoundly helpful to people in recovery even though it lacks support groups or other elements of recovery programming."[19] Imagine what can happen when we use our space, our gifts, and our church family to be a direct means of introducing people who are hurting to the God who heals.

The Ministry of Mending the Broken

Isn't it stunning that for all the research done in science, theology, medicine, psychology, and philosophy, that underneath all the theories, the common theme of addiction is brokenness? Of all things, *this* Christians should understand. But it's not easy to put compassion into practice, even in the context of a church community.

We tend to stop it up with our hang-ups, our fears, our prejudices, and our personal discomfort. I wonder if it's because we don't see ourselves as needing grace. Maybe we've played the polished-to-perfection game for so long, we don't see it. Our standards of holiness are bound to the old covenant, requiring performance, instead of being bound to the new covenant of mercy and grace through the blood of Jesus Christ.[20] Brennan Manning writes:

In order to free us for compassion toward others, Jesus calls us to accept his compassion in our own lives, to become gentle, caring, compassionate, and forgiving toward ourselves in our failure and need. Compassion for others is not a simple virtue because it avoids snap judgments—right or wrong, good or bad, hero or villain: it seeks truth in all its complexity. Genuine compassion means that in empathizing with the failed plans and uncertain love of the other person, we send out the vibration, "Yes, ragamuffin, I understand. I've been there too."[21]

The people who watched in awe as Jesus called Lazarus out of the tomb followed him around until Passover—if they weren't following him already. Jesus, in that one miraculous moment of healing, became the greatest show in town. The miracle was so astonishing and convincing that they held a huge parade for him as he entered Jerusalem for what he knew would be the last time. The crowd believed the Messiah was going to set everything right. Instead, a few days later, they turned on him, spurred on by the Pharisees, and when "The Way" became suffering, they not only abandoned him, but "he was despised and rejected," Isaiah says. "We hid our faces from him."[22]

Too many of us want church to be comfortable. We want it on our terms, as we understand it. But the feast, the party, the parade—this is not where Jesus calls us. He calls us to the people who are despised and rejected like he was. We can either choose to shut out the brokenness and keep the church neat and tidy, or we can open our eyes to the mission that has invaded our communities and threatens lives all around us. Drug addiction is no longer *their* problem. It's *our* problem. We can't move our churches to the suburbs anymore and pretend we're safe from the opioid crisis. It's everywhere.

We live in a charming seaside town of 10,000 people. Even here, we have drug rings, professionals lose their jobs because of addiction, young people in our county have died from overdose. The pervasiveness of the crisis is daunting.

A lot of towns in this country still have a church on every corner. Your church may not be able to run a recovery program. But you can probably point to another church in town that does. If we want to reach broken people in need in our communities, we need to work as a team to remove the division and barriers that keep them from seeing the church as a place to find healing.

seven

The Power of a Support Group

Shame can't survive being spoken. It thrives on secrecy, silence, and judgment. If we can share our experience of shame with someone who responds with empathy, shame can't survive.

BRENÉ BROWN

Confess your sins to each other and pray for each other so that you may be healed.

JAMES 5:16

Shame is a powerful master. It is our oldest, most practiced response to exposure, and it goes all the way back to the garden. Like Adam and Eve, we all react to shame by hiding. What we hide behind depends on how we're wired. Some of us hide behind a strong exterior—tough, loud, aggressive. Some of us duck behind rules and rightness—judgmentalism. Some of us just withdraw from society. How we *wear* our shame depends on our upbringing, faith practice, and education. How we *deal with* our shame depends on these factors plus our personality. Some of us buy the "you're bad" narrative and stick with it, and we give in to our impulses and tell ourselves we can't possibly ever be good. Shame, if we can find it and name it in ourselves, is the place where we need the most healing and the place that shows us our deepest need for grace.[1]

Even if whatever we're ashamed of wasn't our fault, shame has a way of making us feel as though it is. For some of us, shame is such a part of our makeup, we don't even see it. Unlike conviction of sin, or guilt because we've done something wrong, shame wants us to believe we can't possibly be forgiven, erodes our confidence, and promises rejection.

Confession helps to heal us of shame. Sometimes it's owning up to something you've done, and sometimes it's just speaking up about what was done to you. That old word, *confiteri* or *confessio* in Latin, means to acknowledge. We usually think of confession as an admission of guilt, but *speaking up* is at its root. It's hard to speak up when you believe wholeheartedly and perhaps with good reason that you will be judged or rejected, which only leads to more shame.

The Power of a Common Bond

Support groups have a unique purpose. Those that are run well provide a safe place to release the steam that has built up in our hearts under pressure. It's a place to let down our guard without judgment or advice. Groups have been lifelines to sanity for millions of people. We need the encouragement of those who've been through what we're going through, and we can find comfort in the camaraderie of those who are working through it, in the trenches, beside us. Common experience is a powerful bond, and when we find people who "get it," we relax a little. Not having to establish context over and over opens the door to admitting our failures and exposing our hurts for healing. And yet misconception, pride, and skepticism keep some of us from trying out this unique place of healing.

I think the thing that keeps most of us away from support

groups for loved ones of people in addiction and recovery is that we aren't sure we belong there, and frankly, we don't want to belong. We don't feel like we'd fit in with *those people*. I know that's how I felt. Until I went. I knew there would be comfort in a shared common experience, but I didn't want *that* common experience. I didn't want to be "the wife of an addict." Somehow, going to a support group made it all very, very real.

I didn't go until I was off-the-charts angry. I kept going because I needed a safe place to say aloud the things I couldn't yet tell my friends or family. I found some comfort just in knowing I wasn't alone.

In his book *Beautiful Boy: A Father's Journey through His Son's Addiction*, David Sheff recounts some of his experiences attending Al-Anon meetings for families of people struggling with addiction. Sheff's son was addicted to meth, and this father's story is full of love and compassion, confusion, and questions. He admits that he is generally one to avoid meetings where sharing feelings is involved, but just like me, desperation to connect with someone who understood motivated his attendance. He writes:

> I kept our family's problem a secret for a long time. It wasn't that I was ashamed. I wanted to protect Nic—to preserve our friends' and others' good impressions of him. But I have learned that the AA adage is true: you're as sick as your secrets. I have learned how much it helps to talk about my son's addiction and reflect on it and hear and read others' stories. . . .
>
> My first impulse in the meeting is condescension. I look around with something bordering on loathing. . . . By the time I leave, however, I feel an affinity with everyone here—the parents and children and husbands and wives and lovers and brothers and sisters of the drug-addicted. My heart breaks for them.
>
> I am one of them.[2]

Hope rises and falls in the process of addiction recovery. That's the thing so many of us don't realize about it—or maybe we just want to believe that somehow our loved one's experience will be different. Some studies say people who are addicted to drugs relapse an average of seven times before they're done. The statistic was definitely true of Dave.

Looking back, I can see that I should have gone to some sort of support group as soon as I knew Dave had a problem with addiction. But I believed those sorts of groups were for other people, and we did not need them. At first, I talked myself into believing our problem wasn't bad enough to go. Later, after a couple of relapses, I felt so alone I ached for someone who could relate and give me some hope. But I was afraid of judgment. I was afraid of someone thinking poorly of us. And of God. I was afraid word would get around our small town and that it would get back to people at camp or Dave's boss and he'd be fired.

A Safe Place to Share

Support groups are such a part of our culture now that parodies poke fun at them, but bearing each other's burdens and confessing to each other brings healing. When we let God and people we trust into our painful wounds, the work of healing begins. Letting God into a wound often means letting another person or people be an instrument of his grace. We could call this, in fact, a *ministry of healing*. Or *recovery*.

The funny thing is, every person I know who has had a positive experience in a recovery support group says the same thing: *I wish church was like this. I wish someone would speak up in church and just say, "I'm struggling with . . ."* I've been in church when that's happened and it can be awkward. No one knows what to do—it's our instinct to scramble to feel comfortable again. We minimize with "Oh well, we all have problems." Imagine what would happen if the person came back week after week with an update on their struggle. It would take all day to go around a room of a hundred or more people to ask how they've been doing with the thing they brought up last week. Small groups are a better place for that sort of accountability.

But ordinary church small groups have a drawback as well. Even in small groups, quiet people find they have to be fairly assertive to get a word in, and when it's their turn to talk, it's difficult to continue speaking after being interrupted. There are always answer-giving people: *Read this verse. Study this book. You know, what you ought to do is* . . . Members of Bible studies and small groups can lapse into bad manners in part because they know each other or are used to each other. When you are already feeling broken and vulnerable, Bible study prayer request time can be brutal. It's important to hold space for someone to cry, let out their hurts, or ask for prayer without offering immediate advice. The next time you are in a small group situation, whether at work or church or in the broader community, notice how the talkers dominate group discussions or brainstorming sessions. Quiet people, or people who are reticent about speaking their thoughts (aka deeply hurt people), may need an invitation—or at least the opportunity—to speak. That's what "holding space" means in a group setting.

When I'm hurting, I am more likely to speak up in an environment that doesn't make me shout to be heard like I'm playing a game of Pit. One-on-one conversations? Sure, I'm up for that. Group talk in which the loudest gets the most attention? No thank you. Loudest person dominance of a group is the verbal equivalent of the James passage in which we save the best seats in church for the best dressed among us. The most outgoing or gregarious talkers are the ones who are heard. A support group that requires taking turns eliminates dominance and sets an expectation of holding space for hurting people who don't feel safe speaking their pain out loud in other places.

When a wound is buried deep and covered with a layer of shame, you may have to allow it time to work its way to the surface, like a splinter on the bottom of your foot. You just keep soaking it or putting soothing hot compresses on it until the skin ejects the splinter. The comfort and security of a support group can help us open up about hurts that are causing us to limp through life.

A Safe Place to Fall

—H DAVE—

But support groups aren't just a safe place to share. They're also a place for accountability—a place to say, "I really messed up this week." In a 12 Step recovery group, we are "working the steps," which means practicing what we are learning.

At a Christ-based 12 Step group, the main meeting involves speaking and then "breakout" groups, which are support groups. The step work intensifies in study groups, which involve questions for study and discussion. In these group times, participants work through each step, breaking it down into smaller sections, and are asked deeper, more targeted questions. In a Christ-based recovery group, these step studies will involve specific biblical principles, Scripture readings, and verses that go along with each step. We memorized Scripture too and applied some hard verses that pointed us to Jesus as our higher power.

At each meeting in an AA group, we read through the 12 steps and group guidelines (just as in CR) and then have a testimony or talk about one of the steps. People come for accountability, support, or because they are part of a program that requires or encourages them to attend.

But in Christ-based groups, there's also a focus on Jesus, who was *tempted in every way*, who suffered and died, *taking all the decrees and judgments against us and nailing them to the cross.* He was raised by the power of God, who also raises us and fills us with the Holy Spirit who empowers us to live and bear the crosses laid on us.

Many people are familiar with the beginning of the Serenity Prayer: "God, grant me the serenity to accept the things I cannot change; the courage to change the things I can; and the wisdom to know the difference." But they don't know the rest of it, and that's where the grit of it comes in:

> Living one day at a time,
> enjoying one moment at a time;
> accepting hardship as a pathway to peace;
> taking, as Jesus did,
> this sinful world as it is,
> not as I would have it;
> trusting that You will make all things right
> if I surrender to Your will;
> so that I may be reasonably happy in this life
> and supremely happy with You forever in the next.
> Amen.[3]

It's all about following the example of Christ.

In the end, after the Serenity Prayer, people will tell each other to keep coming back. All of this takes the 12 Steps beyond the "Hi, my name is Dave" caricatures we see in entertainment media.

A Safe Place to Heal

The recovery process is most effective when our reasons for addiction, destructive behaviors, or shame are addressed. Some of our heartaches work their way to the surface over years with a trusted friend. Some stay with us to the grave. And some, maybe the ones we're secretly carrying, exercise a power over us that keeps us from moving forward in our lives. The beauty of a good support group is that it becomes a safe place to talk and experience the power of testimony. Hearing each other's stories and telling our own brings light into our darkness.

The part of Washington where we live is notorious for rain. It's so common, if you didn't go out in it, you wouldn't do anything. But once, when we went camping, it rained so hard and the kids were so miserable, we finally decided to just pack it in and go to a hotel. Our kids were small, so we put them in the minivan and packed up our gear. There was no way to keep the tent dry while we folded it up, so we just wrapped it up, shoved it under a seat in the van, and continued on our vacation.

When we got home several days later and unpacked, the tent was as smelly as you would expect. So we asked an outdoorsy friend what sort of spray cleaner was best for cleaning out a tent, and he said just to set it up in sunshine and let the breeze go through it. Airing it out in the warm sun for a few days returned the tent to a normal campy smell. That's what recovery support groups are like. You unwrap the tent you tucked away with all the mess in it to deal with later, set it up, and let it air out.

The power of testimony does two things: saying something out loud makes it real. The impact can hit us hard but doesn't destroy us. Then our turn is done and the next person speaks up and they're not burned to a crisp. We don't hate them, we don't attack them. And we are not destroyed, not attacked, not hated.

The first time I went to a support group was in rehab. Up to that point, I thought AA was either the auto club or a cult! Instead I found it to be the most powerful part of rehab. Because here were some people who looked homeless and some who were white-collar professionals and we all admitted—just by showing up—that we had a problem. People would tell personal, difficult, often embarrassing stories, and at the end, the only comment was "Thank you for sharing." There was no advice given, no corrective action or assignments, except to keep coming back. Not everyone who attends a 12 Step meeting sees its power right away, but this type of sharing impacted me immediately. Telling my secret shame was such a huge burden off my shoulders. It wasn't an instant fix, and I quit going after a few months and didn't go back for several years because I thought I could handle it myself and didn't want to admit I wasn't fixed.

After we were introduced to CR, and Deb went with me to meetings, I was reminded of the value of support groups and the freedom I felt among people who were okay with my recovery being "in process." Every other place I went wanted me to be fixed already. People loved the "fixed already" testimony. "I used to be . . ." and everyone claps. This time, I began actually working through the steps in a step study group. There was something powerful to me about being around other Christians who were admitting their struggles and working together toward healing. It helped me be more honest—*we are all struggling, but we are still believers.*

I've never been to a support group meeting and regretted going, not even a little. The accountability is not from jumping through hoops (as I understood it previously); the accountability was in *trying.* I didn't have to prove I was better; I just needed to be there. There wasn't an expectation that because you'd confessed your issue the problem was solved. I relapsed twice while I was in that first year of Celebrate Recovery. The second relapse had serious consequences. But the 12 Steps were a major part of my recovery. In a support group there was room to grow. And realizing I was not alone, not the only one with problems who needed help working through them, was powerful in transforming my life.

———⁂———

The first time I (Deb) spoke up in a recovery meeting, I got a little taste of freedom. For five minutes, I spoke without being interrupted, without being corrected, without being advised. I said my piece, the group responded with "thank you," and we moved on to the next person. I had never experienced that sort of listening in my life. Listening not to have a ready answer but to allow a person to break free from darkness. Listening was about standing by as witness to what was happening in a person's heart as God spoke to them. That group of strangers heard things from me that I had never told anyone. In that little group, the bandages were removed from my mouth so I could breathe.

Within a few weeks of that meeting, I moved from a general open-share group to a smaller, regular, committed, and closed group of about eight women, the majority of whom were either married to or adult children of someone who struggled with a serious addiction. I needed the extra layer of safety and security of a closed group because I was so concerned that in seeking help for myself, I would bring disaster on my home. This fear had successfully kept me from seeking help from groups like Al-Anon or Nar-Anon when I first discovered Dave's addiction.

For someone like me, who tended to keep everything bottled inside, working through the questions in the step study group was the most powerful thing I'd ever been a part of. All of us were being asked and answering the same questions. After weeks of just showing up and reading my written answers out loud, I began to trust my group a little more. And that was only possible for me in a place where taking turns was strictly enforced. I would have stopped sharing if I was talked over or interrupted before I finished my slow sentences. I didn't need book recommendations. What I needed most was to stop covering my festering wounds, expose them, and begin the healing process.

Witnessing Change

Bearing witness to the transformation of people who are farther into their recovery than you are is life-giving—and not just for recovering addicts. I didn't know how much I needed encouragement until I was there among other wives and adult children of addicts who were either still in active addiction or working their way through recovery. Though many groups are built around specific issues, the group Dave and I attended could only divide as specifically as gender: men to one group, women to another. That meant my group had women who also struggled with an addiction of some sort.

This group was pivotal for me. Half of the women were dealing with the collateral damage done by their own or their parents' addictions. And the other half of the women were all committed to their husbands, who were addicts in recovery like Dave. They were willing to give them a chance, willing to let them work their program, but shockingly honest about the pain of the process. We worked through the 12 Steps together, those in recovery from addiction and those going along for the awful ride. In that group I learned to embrace compassion for my husband, offer forgiveness, and examine my own life. I had a community of women who understood, listened, and were honest about their own struggles. And, they kept it confidential.

What to Expect from a Support Group

—⊣ DAVE —

This chapter isn't about running a support group, but we want to give you an idea of how support groups work and how valuable they can be for people in addiction recovery and for their loved ones.

And a note: Visit a few groups before deciding where you fit. Go back several times and get used to the flow of the meeting if you've never been to a support group before. You should not feel pressure to share in the first meeting; however, that is the point of a support group. Even after we knew we wanted to go to Celebrate Recovery, it took us a while to find one where we felt like we fit. I tell people who visit our Life Path groups (our church's recovery program, based on Salem Alliance's Life Path program in Oregon) that they should come back a few times before deciding whether it's right for them. This year, our women's group has been working through six-week NACR (National Association for Christian Recovery) studies while my men's group worked through J. Keith Miller's *Hunger for Healing*.

While recovery support groups are not homogenous, all groups have various forms of and perhaps a few additions to these guidelines, but in 12 Step types of groups, they're all essentially the same. Many of these guidelines are just Christian "one anothers" that have been retooled and repackaged into a short list to read every week.

You are free to talk without being interrupted, including being free to cry. It's incredibly difficult for most of us to sit quietly while someone talks through their pain and tears. It's an exercise in self-discipline. But it's critical to understand that a support group is just one part of the whole picture of their recovery. It may actually be the only place where they can freely say what's on their heart. Sometimes people slip into habits of immediately trying to fix the problem, even in a support group. It's a hard habit to break.

It's important to have a good leader who keeps members from slipping into those habits, from taking up too much time, or from using their time to talk about someone else. This can be tricky and it requires tact, firmness, and grace. In 12 Step groups, guidelines are read at the beginning of every meeting so that everyone is reminded of them, but people get to talking and forget, or it's so normal for them to focus on someone else: blaming, faultfinding, or deflecting. It takes time and compassion and sometimes admonition from the group leader to keep them focused on their own issues.

Share about you. It's not intended to be a dump session where you unload about people; it's a place to talk about how *you're* doing. It's not about gossip; it's about what's going on inside you. The tendency, especially at first, is to talk about people or to blame others for our problems. We fumble for a while as we sort out what's happening in our lives. Often a new participant will spend their turn talking about backstory—who the addicted person is, or how they've messed up, how angry they are—and that's okay. It takes time to cut through the surface to the heart, so patience with group members is really important.

We don't give you advice, counseling, or referrals. The 12 Step groups are usually run by laymen, not professional counselors. We always say at our group that "no one is here in a professional capacity." It's all about listening. It's Job, lamenting in front of his gathered friends and hashing things out with God while they sit and listen in silence. We do not know how God is working in a person's heart. In this space, for this moment, they don't need advice or telling. Job's friends had great answers! But in the end, God scolds them: "Who is this that darkens counsel by words without knowledge?"[4] God himself answers Job. You can trust that God will answer you and the person across from you.

Some people don't understand what makes a supportive environment. In a support group, we're not there to teach, mother, or discipline. We're there to speak up. And listen. Too often, we listen so we can respond, so we can have a ready answer. But people often work out their own problems or see what they need to see—sometimes they just need to say it aloud to examine their thoughts. If you can master the discipline of listening in a support group, you will become a healing presence in another person's life. And with practice, you'll become a better listener in your daily interactions as well. It takes self-control, focus, and selflessness to be a good listener.

We keep what you say, and even your presence at the meeting, confidential unless you've threatened to harm yourself or someone else. Anonymity is a tradition for 12 Step groups, Christian or not. There are a myriad of reasons someone may not want their presence in a recovery group broadcast, but the practice of keeping things confidential is intended to be a safeguard against gossip. Some members could lose their job if their struggle is made public. There are recovery groups for nurses, for pastors, for military members and others whose jobs could be in jeopardy if they admitted to anyone they had a problem with addiction. Their attendance in a recovery group doesn't necessarily mean they are using or in active addiction. It just means they need a safe outlet where they can be fully transparent about things they struggle with and give and receive support and encouragement.

We avoid triggers. Not all recovery groups are safe spaces. Sometimes people are too graphic and descriptive of their addiction or about their traumatic life experiences. If you are vulnerable to suggestion or uncomfortable with discussing certain types of trauma (e.g., childhood sexual abuse), a closed group with strict sharing guidelines may be a better fit for you. There are also groups for only men and only women. Some women who've been involved in prostitution for drugs or who have been abused don't feel safe in a mixed group, even if it's just the main group time and not open share. A group is only effective if you feel safe.

For most of us who've kept people—and even God—out of our internal closets, drawing us out is a process. But a good support group leader ensures it's a safe space to let people into our lives. Over time, as trust is built, we open up more. And when we speak up, the secret shame that has buried us loses its power.

Called to Supportive Community

A support group is only one component of a community around the person struggling to overcome addiction or who is married to (or the child of or parent of) someone who has struggled or is struggling with addiction. It may be a starting point, or it may continue to be part of their healing journey. Sometimes members of a support group are just there to give back, to be the support for someone else the way others were a support for them. This is a necessary and important ministry.

Underneath the manifestation of the addiction, the same brokenness runs through each of us. The same gaping chasm of need. We've all tried to fill it in some way, whether with anger, or food, or success, or alcohol, or sex, or drugs—we get it. This is the place to find that common ground of truth and not look at one addiction as worse or easier than another. Someday you will be able to offer hope to another person in your place. There is comfort and encouragement when you gather with people who are going through the same struggles as you.

You can use your past experience to listen with an empathy no one else in a broken person's life can muster. You've been there, and by your very presence in the room, it is evident that you are a survivor. You have lived through something that right now they think they can't. They need you. In your honesty and transparency, you can minister healing to another person. Once people know a little of where you've been, even the simple statement, "Hi, my name is Dave. I've been clean from pills for ten years now, and today was a good day," speaks volumes to the guy who can't imagine staying sober for an entire week.

———— ‖ ————

Too many of us want to leave the past in the past. We take Paul's words "forgetting what lies behind"[5] to mean we should never look back, when he meant for us not to rest on our accomplishments, in how smart we are, on our good choices, or on our successes, spiritual or otherwise. Instead, he calls us to remember that "such were some of you"[6] and to recall the grace we've received and to comfort one another with the same comfort with which we have been comforted.[7] We can take the grace given to us and pass it on to others. This may be the most powerful and effective ministry we can have in our lives: *Here is where I was. You are not alone. Here is what God did for me. There is reason to hope.*

· · · · · · · ·

There are times, however, when a support group is not the right fit or it will not offer enough help for us and we need professional intervention. This is true not only for an addict in recovery but for their parent, spouse, or child as well.

eight

The Healing Effect of Counseling

> Secular education today is aware that often a person can be helped merely by having someone who will listen to him seriously, and upon this insight it has constructed its own soul therapy, which has attracted great numbers of people, including Christians.
>
> DIETRICH BONHOEFFER

In October of 2018, PBS's *Nova* featured an episode contrasting the failures of punitive opioid addiction recovery methods with compassionate recovery care. Dr. Bessel van der Kolk, author of *The Body Keeps the Score*, appears in the episode and emphasizes the place of trauma in addiction. Van der Kolk says, "Trauma is an experience that overwhelms you, that leaves you bereft, paralyzed and with no way out. What you're left with, as a kid, is these heartbreaking feelings of 'I'm no good,' and 'The world is a terrible place.' Somebody says to you, 'Here is something that will make these feelings go away.' And so, people take drugs, because they can't stand the way they feel."[1]

Not everyone who's struggled with addiction had serious childhood trauma, but Dr. Daniel Sumrok, director of the Center for

Addiction Sciences at the University of Tennessee, says Adverse Childhood Experiences, or ACEs, play a powerful role in shaping addictive behavior.[2] ACEs include being abused, witnessing your mother being abused, substance abuse in your home, mental illness in your home, parental separation or divorce, a household member in prison, or emotional and physical neglect under the age of eighteen.[3] What Dr. Sumrok found in his studies was that substance abusers (addicts) tend to have higher ACE scores, meaning they experienced some form of serious childhood trauma.

People abuse drugs for a reason. Unfortunately, the consequences cause more trauma. When someone who has been struggling with addiction finally lets go of the crutch or cover provided by their substance of choice, it can be a difficult, slow, painful walk to freedom. On the outside, to family and friends, this stage of recovery can be troubling. Maybe we're not seeing the external progress we think we should be seeing. But so much is happening in their bodies and brains and hearts at once. And at some point, they will begin to address the *why* of their addiction. Digging into the *why* often brings up buried pain and forces them to unwrap more of themselves, releasing a not-so-pleasing aroma, like airing out Lazarus's bandages.

J. Keith Miller, author of *A Hunger for Healing: The Twelve Steps as a Classic Model for Christian Spiritual Growth*, says, "To alleviate the pain and fear of our bruised relationships and our powerlessness, we often engage in compulsive behaviors. . . . This is what addictive behavior is about—covering our intense pain so we don't have to feel it."[4]

For Dave, the prescription pills he abused leveled him out and gave him a sense of confidence when he felt weak. They kept him from facing pain head-on, for one, but they also kept him from feeling insecurities that plagued him—feelings that were easily numbed by a handful of pills.

I don't know anyone who doesn't numb themselves to pain in some way. Perhaps it's Tylenol for a tooth that's been bugging us. To get a break from emotional pain or stress, we might binge watch a show on Netflix or read a steady stream of romance novels, immersing ourselves in imaginary relationships. Maybe it's running—it seems healthy and positive, but the music flowing through the earbuds and the rhythm of our feet on the pavement have become an obsession and a place to escape thought. Anything good can be twisted into sustained escape from the reality of our lives past, present, and future.

On the surface, you may think you detect resistance or even indifference, but inside them, there's a war going on: physical, mental, spiritual. The early stages of breaking free from anything that has a grip on the soul isn't pretty. I know this is true of me. Some days, in counseling, I talked with my counselor about things I'd buried because I didn't want to deal with them. For a time, I went through something much like grief as I came to see how much of my life had been hindered by what I thought I'd buried. Turns out I'd been dragging it around with me instead.

The discomfort of dealing with old wounds is much like the itchiness you feel when a bone is healing, isn't it? But that horrible discomfort, as contrary as it seems to our common sense, is a sign that the bone is really healing. And sometimes, if the bone healed wrong the first time, they might have to rebreak and reset it. Either way, there is plenty of pain and discomfort in the process of healing your physical body. And there's plenty of pain and discomfort when our hearts and souls are healing. If you haven't healed properly, if you've just covered up the old wounds instead of allowing healing into them, there's going to be pain when you reset your life.

Counseling for the Person in Recovery

—{ DAVE —

Don't assume that because you are free from the pills, your spirit will always be free from temptation or from the triggers that would send you spiraling backward. Sometimes, we're not ready to address past wounds right away. But at some point, people in addiction recovery benefit from counseling, because as Melody Beattie, author of *Codependent No More*, writes, "Sobriety is not a magical cure for anger and relationship problems."[5]

Not all counselors or methods are the same or provide the same level of care. Addiction recovery counselors/specialists have completed additional coursework, training, and certification beyond their licensed mental health counselor certification. We've found that counselors who specialize in trauma are also good at getting below the surface of addictive behaviors and digging into the *reasons why*.

The critical role of a counselor is not simply to get a person battling addiction to stop using but to get to the root of addictive, self-destructive behavior. This is important because if they do not deal with the root of the problem, it will resurface and result in relapse or it will manifest in a different way. Addiction carries with it a load of shame, but a compassionate and competent counselor can, over time, address the reasons for addiction and help people in recovery move toward new patterns of behavior.

There are physical reasons for relapse that have nothing to do with a psychological one. An injury, for example, can become a prime opportunity for relapse. Apart from these physical triggers, a good counselor can help you uncover more deeply rooted issues that resurface when certain things happen. For example, maybe you turn to alcohol when social situations are uncomfortable and you've been doing this for years. A counselor will help you get to the root of why social situations make you so uncomfortable and help you find strategies to cope with the situation that are not self-destructive.

My experiences with counseling are somewhat different from Deb's. I'm a talker by nature, so once I was forced to quit keeping my addiction secret, I was pretty much an open book. Counseling was rough when I was still trying to control my addiction myself. Though I met weekly with a counselor, I went back to using within a few months. I did that twice, a few years apart. It's not very productive to see a counselor when you are deceiving them too.

——— JJ ———

Counseling for Family

There is emotional trauma in loving a broken person. There is a limp you will live with. There is learning—or relearning—what a "normal" relationship is. Learning a new way of relating to each other might require professional help.

Psychology categorizes our responses to trauma with flight, fight, or freeze. All of us do one of these to some extent, but in intense trauma, we push even harder into one of those patterns of response. J. D. Vance writes about this in his memoir, *Hillbilly Elegy*:

> For kids like me, the part of the brain that deals with stress and conflict is always activated—the switch flipped indefinitely. We are constantly ready to fight or flee, because there is a constant exposure to the bear, whether that bear is an alcoholic dad or an unhinged mom. We become hardwired for conflict. And that wiring remains, even when there's no more conflict to be had.[6]

As spouses or parents or children of someone who struggled with addiction, it's likely that we have residual anger and fear, among other feelings. And we may have become reactionary rather than nurturing or compassionate toward our loved one. It can be healing to turn to an expert for help for yourself as you walk beside someone in recovery. At the very least, working on our own issues keeps us from obsessing about theirs!

It took me a long time to understand that part of my struggle with Dave's addiction was a crisis of identity. In my world, a Christian wife was supposed to be submissive to her husband, but my husband was addicted to pills. I couldn't reconcile what my behavior and response should be.

A Good Counselor Addresses Overfunctioning

Some of us realize too, or maybe had it pointed out to us, that we were helping our loved one continue in their bad behavior. It might take a trusted counselor to help us see where we are doing this. Obvious examples include buying beer for an alcoholic husband so that he'll be pleasant, lying to your child's boss when they are too high to drive to work, shielding your sister from the consequences of her actions by dropping everything over and over to come bail her out when she's drunk. It might be important for you to stop overfunctioning—consistently doing things for someone that they can do for themselves. Overfunctioning is often called "enabling."

The trouble with applying the label "enabler" to people in the prescription drug addict's life is that the lines aren't nearly as clear as they are with other addictions. Picking up your dad's prescription for him because he just had surgery and can't drive is hardly enabling. Encouraging your spouse to call in sick when they're experiencing the side effects of pain pills for migraines isn't enabling. And bailing out your son whose struggle with pain has left him with massive medical debt isn't necessarily enabling either. We don't look at pain medication—prescribed by a doctor—the same way we look at heroin or even alcohol.

Conversely, when someone is engaging in behaviors you know are destructive, but you stand by and support them financially and even emotionally, you might be enabling. But when they are engaging in behavior that's legal, and especially when they are chronically ill, it's extremely difficult to pinpoint what is enabling and what is simply caring for an ill person. For years I thought I was sacrificially helping a sick husband, but it turned out I was overfunctioning for an addict. It was so helpful for me to talk through compassion, guilt, anger, and reconciliation with a counselor, even years later.

This is what happens to some of us who have gotten used to relating to our spouse or loved one in ways that we were not intended to. I was not Dave's parent, but in some ways, when he was struggling with addiction, I took on that role. Learning to acknowledge and recognize his growth in recovery and begin to see him as my partner again, rather than someone I had to supervise, took some painful adjustment. Restoring trust takes deliberate practice, and for me, it also took professional help.

A Good Counselor Addresses Destructive Patterns

Our oldest boy broke his arm when he was five. He was at a friend's house after church, riding a bike in his long-sleeved, button-down Sunday best when he fell. He didn't cry, but our friends called because it seemed like something was wrong, and he did not want them to touch his arm. Our doctor's office was closed, so Dave was sent back and forth across town to find help at an open urgent care. Then there was the waiting to be seen. The poor kid sat motionless, tearless, and probably in shock.

When someone finally took off his shirt hours later (a move that induced tears) to put his arm on the table for an X-ray, everyone was stunned. He had a compound fracture just above the elbow. The shattered bone had nearly pierced through his skin!

Off to a hospital, to surgery. Worries about growth plates, placement of pins, and possibilities of permanent damage swirled. I spent a sleepless night beside him in the hospital, marveling at his pain tolerance, grieving that he had suffered so much all that horrible long day—nine hours in all before the relief of anesthesia. I was amazed a small child could absorb so much pain without a word.

I'll never forget the conference I had with his kindergarten teacher nearly a year later and our discussion about my son's writing. I hadn't noticed my right-handed boy had learned to write, somewhat poorly, with his left hand. Instead of working his damaged right arm, he compensated with his left. But because he was naturally right-handed, he had to be retrained to use his right hand to write.

When we are broken, we sometimes learn to compensate for our weakness or pain in ways that are not how we were designed to function. When this happens, we have to relearn better coping skills, and a counselor can help us do that.

A Good Counselor Addresses the Pain of Past Regrets

There's an interesting guilt that hit both of us at midlife. As each of us, from a point of better health all around, looked back at different patterns in our lives, we found it was easy to slip into regrets. The kids are all growing and leaving home, so there's a bit of a sadness there anyway. The past hits you hard sometimes, and sorting through boxes of pictures of your children will do that. *Here's when Daddy was not at my birthday because he was in rehab.* Or *Wow, Mom sounds so old and crabby on that video.* Or realizing you don't know your kids' friends' parents so well because you were consumed with your own problems for the entire decade they were in school. These are the sort of things that come back to you in waves, long after the last pill. And they are the sort of things that send former addicts back to addiction. It was good for both of us to see counselors, separately, to talk through the pieces of the past that were causing us pain. Good counselors ask great questions. They listen well. And they teach us to use tools we didn't know we needed but are so grateful for.

· · · · · · · ·

Tips for surviving when a family member is in counseling:

- Be aware that as a person deals with things they've stuffed down for years, the pain works its way to the surface and it may be difficult to deal with.
- Communicate with each other. Even something like "It was a rough day in counseling" can help prevent potential conflict.

- Wash dishes by hand. There's something soothing about immersing your hands in hot water. (I know this sounds strange here, but it's true.) Or do some other mindless but productive chore.
- Make allowance for each other's faults.
- Not all counselors are the right fit. If your desire and goal in counseling, for example, is to stay married and work through the side effects of addiction, you'll want to find a counselor who agrees with your goal.

nine

The Role of Rehab

> It doesn't make sense for people to go through rehab only to have them return to communities that fail to support their recovery.
>
> ANN M. FLETCHER

Popular reality shows like *Intervention* make it seem as though our primary focus as loved ones of someone battling addiction is to get them into rehab. We come away from watching with the idea that if we can just get them into rehab, they'll be fine. But the reality is, rehab may be just a step—and a step they may have to repeat a few times. Viewing rehab as the cure-all for addiction leads to unrealistic expectations and may push us to despair after a "failure" like relapse or dropping out of the program. Rather than considering rehab as success or failure, we need to see it as another step in the journey. Rehabs, or residential recovery programs, are just a piece of the puzzle.

Detox vs. Rehab

The single greatest difficulty with a long-term recovery program is the expectation that completing a program means total healing.

An inpatient recovery program can be a worthwhile and valuable start. And the longer you stay clean, the greater your chances of long-term success, but graduating from a program does not mean the end of recovery.

—{ DAVE —

A lot of people confuse detox with rehab. When I went to a three-week inpatient rehab in a county hospital, it was really only long enough to get me through acute withdrawal, or detox. As I recounted earlier, I'd been taking thirty pills a day when I went in and was so physically dependent on Tramadol, they had to put me back on the drug and slowly wean me off with the help of sedatives. I was violently ill or fairly out of it for most of those three weeks. While the program also included exercise, counseling, and meetings, overall it was merely an introduction to recovery. In our sessions together, the focus was on learning the work of recovery and tools for building and maintaining sobriety. They recommended attending ninety meetings (12 Step recovery meetings) in ninety days when I got out. In other words, I should go to a meeting every day for the next three months. They didn't promise a three-week cure. It was intended to be a beginning and not an end. At rehab, they told me, "It took you ten years to get here, you're not going to get out and be healed."

In my mind, however, I had visions of my great-grandfather who, according to family history, stopped drinking the moment he came to Jesus. I thought maybe this was my "come to Jesus" moment, but instead of one night at a revival meeting, it was three weeks in rehab. I only went to a few meetings when I got out of rehab. And by ninety days out, I had relapsed.

Perhaps because the term "rehab" is applied to so many different types of programs, our expectation of them is the same. A month in a rehab unit isn't a cure. They know most of us will be back. The value in short-term stays is a longer time in detox (rather than just a couple of nights in a detox facility) and personalized, specific guidance on *how to start a life in recovery*. Places like the one I was in, with 21- to 28-day programs, are for people not willing or able to do or pay for a long-term stay in treatment.

———— ⸭ ————

The Rehab Business

One misunderstood piece of the recovery process is the effectiveness of, or even need for, rehab. Inpatient or residential treatment programs can range from three weeks to two years. As of this writing, there's no single national standard for recovery businesses or nonprofits to comply with when it comes to recovery.[1] "Rehab" can mean a sober living facility or aversion therapy sessions or outpatient methadone treatment, or dozens of other types of programs. Some that are effective for alcohol are not effective for opioids or pills. It's important to remember that rehab programs are not all the same. There are no national standards, there is no oversight, and the business is rife with corruption.

Today addiction treatment is a $35 billion industry. Rehab websites look slick and authoritative like they're the Mayo Clinic, but most are privately run businesses. A thirty-day residential stay in a private facility can cost $30,000 to $100,000.[2] Some programs are run like boot camp in hopes of instilling good discipline and habits; others, like a luxury spa. There are also scams. Some that prey mercilessly on addicts, treating them to claim insurance money and dumping them back on the street in the path of hired dealers, creating a cash flow.

Even highly respected programs make grand promises and advertise good results, but it's important to remember that every rehab has the same basic success rate. They simply measure differently. Long-term, inpatient recovery programs typically measure success rates by their graduates and rarely report the number of addicts who enter their program and don't complete it. That's a big difference. Former Secretary of Health, Education, and Welfare and founder of the National Center on Addiction and Substance Abuse Joseph Califano says, "The therapeutic community claims a 30% success rate, but they only count people who complete the program. Seventy to eighty percent drop out in three to six months."[3]

In addition, program success rates don't take into account all the times an addict tried to get clean and even tried rehab before, or circumstances and life changes that made this time different. The truth: when someone gets clean and it lasts, we attribute success to the last thing they tried—be it a program, a prayer, or therapy—rather than looking at all the pieces that may have worked together, many times, over years, to get them clean.

We can see, looking back over fifteen years now, that all the things Dave did, we did, and God did worked together. We're not professionals and cannot recommend specific treatment for your loved one. Rehab may be exactly right for them. But it's important to remember rehab is just a part of the whole picture.

Critical Detox

Many long-term inpatient or residential recovery programs (rehab) require addicts to be clean for a certain number of days before entering their program. This time requirement ranges from days to months and is set by the program. The good thing about the delineation between "detox" and "rehab" is that there is a clear expectation set out at the beginning. Each part of the process is a separate step.

Going into a rehab program that does not have a medically supervised and assisted detox can be life-threatening. A qualified addiction professional can help you and your loved one find the right sequence and timing and determine with you what sort of program is best. Initial detox can take anywhere from a weekend to a month, or more, depending on the amount of drugs, the strength of them, and the years you've been taking them. The higher the amount being taken and tolerated, the worse the withdrawal from them. Whether in a detox center or tapering off pills at home, withdrawal and detox should be done under medical supervision.

But the problem with a detox requirement for admission to a rehab program is that the period between getting clean and getting into a program can be too big of a window for some and they may relapse. If someone is ready to get clean, it may not be wise or healthy to make them wait on a waiting list for the "perfect program." People can relapse in that time. A friend of ours was on a waiting list for a long-term specialized outpatient program that would help him keep his job, but having failed before, he didn't wait to start the process of recovery. He started going to local 12 Step meetings and reached out for multiple sources of help staying clean in the interim so that he didn't fall backward while waiting. A lot of addicts cannot do this waiting period without help. In other words, when someone tells you they're ready to get clean, don't make them get on a waiting list for a program! Tap into community resources and let them get started.

The Benefits of Long-Term Residential Programs

—{ DAVE —

In rehab, often separate from detox, patients will begin to face the reasons they turned to drugs or alcohol—or started abusing their legitimate prescriptions—to cope with their lives or to get high. Rehab is just the beginning of a long process of retraining the addict to live in a more healthy way. We can't expect our loved one to come home completely "fixed" any more than we can expect a person who's broken bones in an accident to be "fixed" when they are released from the hospital. Even though rehab isn't the end of the recovery process, there are many benefits to going into one. These benefits can be found in low-cost programs like state hospitals and recovery ranches. Rehab doesn't need to drive your family further into debt.

Time. Every day of sobriety increases the chances of staying sober for a person in addiction recovery. Past ninety days, their chances go up exponentially. This is why the common minimum for a long-term rehab program is ninety days.

Distance. For some addicts, it's critical to be removed completely from the people with whom they've gotten into trouble. For others, being cut off from every other responsibility in their lives helps them to focus solely on sobriety and recovery.

A safe place. When an addict's home or lifestyle means exposure to drugs and abuse, or when rehab is an alternative to jail or they've been involved in gang activity, crime, or close relationships with people who are using drugs, their best chance of successful recovery may be total removal from their community or environment.

Specialized care. In rehab, they should receive counseling, professional analysis, personalized assistance, and a full tool kit to come out and keep working at recovery. Many rehab programs incorporate steady physical work, Bible studies, and group counseling. (I still use information and skills I learned from rehab, even though I relapsed afterward.) For others, a year or two of reworking the ruts and grooves in their lives that have been created over years of addiction and broken relationships helps them to heal from their addiction.

The downside of long-term rehab, of course, is separation.

The Pitfalls of Rehab

In America we want a professional to fix all our problems. A pastor to talk to my kid. A school to get them into college. A counselor to deal with a husband. A program to make the addiction problem go away. But recovery is not something we can turn over to the professionals and be done with.

The trouble with rehab programs is the same trouble we have as a society for those who get out of prison or return from a war: *reentry and reunification*. How do you work your way back into the larger community of family, church, work, and so forth? Too often, we just expect them to leave the protected environment, be healed, and jump right back in.

Addiction is devastating for a family, and separation alone does not heal relationships. If the person going through rehab is married, eventually they'll come home and try to work through a life in recovery together. Though relationship work may have begun on the recovering addict's end of things, even if the long-term program involved some family reunification days and counseling, they still must deal with reentry into the life of the family.

We work in an area with military, and one of the things they actively prepare for is the rough reentry into family life for both the serviceperson of a long deployment and their family. Absence may make the heart grow fonder—or it can make us think we might be better off without the complications or responsibilities the other person brings to our life. Their absence places a heavy burden on the one still at home, especially if there are children. In rehab, Dave was getting all sorts of positive affirmation and I was cleaning up the mess he'd made that sent him there. I didn't get any of the benefits of rehab Dave was getting: no counseling, no personalized care. He walked back into our home still fragile, and I was ready for him to get a job and be my husband and a great dad again. I didn't want his words of amends. I just wanted him to be better.

If we, as a family member, are not expecting that our loved one will have to keep working on recovery and that the recovery work may also involve us, we may unwittingly throw up an obstacle for their long-term success. The first time Dave came out of rehab, I was determined to believe and act as though he was fixed. Years later, when he came home from his parents' house after detoxing on their couch out of my sight—and throwing range—I knew he wasn't cured. He might have been clean from the drugs, but our life still needed work. This time, I knew better than to expect Super Dad and husband to rise like a phoenix from the ashes like I did before. If we were going to stay together, I had no choice but to face "one day at a time, one moment at a time," just like he did.

The Need for Residential Family Programs

Rescue mission recovery programs fill a massive need, usually because they're free to participants. Their programs, too, vary. While most can only accommodate singles, some rescue missions have embraced the long-term value of keeping families together. There is a cost to a family of removing the chief breadwinner, and the toll the disruption takes on the kids does not lead to long-term family health. These programs provide stability for the entire family and often include classes and job training for parents, along with daycare for children. Rescue missions used to be considered for the addict only, but these ministries recognize whole families need to be healed from the wounds of addiction. In addition, the cycle of addiction is commonly repeated in a family. The goal of family-based rescue ministries is to break the cycle of homelessness by addressing the underlying causes, like addiction, and bringing true healing.

Entering a residential recovery program may mean giving up your job (unless you can get a leave of absence—always check your employee benefits) and separation from your family. That's why whole family recovery programs have become increasingly effective. Families who've experienced the devastating loss of income need stability in order for the user not to relapse into addiction. Falling into relapse while you're trying to rebuild your family and life is demoralizing. If the spouse cannot support them with his or her income, supplemental aid is necessary. That's part of the benefit of a residential family program—resetting at zero instead of spending miserable years on the edge. The full program, from entry through counseling and care—sometimes medical, dental, clothes, hair, food, childcare—is a fully supportive environment while you get back on your feet as a family and financially.

The Power of Healing in Our Own Community

In hindsight, I have wished that we'd known about and had the humility to apply for one of these long-term programs. What we needed was a place to learn how to be self-sufficient, we needed counseling, and we needed childcare so I could return to work. What a blessed freedom it would have been that first time out of rehab for Dave to have found a normal job to support us, to drop out of seminary, to move to a place where housing was more affordable, to have the recovery from addiction at number one on our priority list—rather than jumping back into ministry.

When Dave finally broke free, he had to manage both detox and rehab with only a few weeks off regular work. He did, however, take a job that required intense accountability with his time, he went to weekly 12 Step meetings, met with our pastor, and met with his sponsor. In essence, he was in a long-term recovery program that disrupted our regular routines, *but* he was contributing to our family *and* establishing healthy patterns at work, at home, and in recovery—working all sides, all at once.

This is where compassionate community, educated in the needs of families in recovery, can play a powerful role. Not just one church. Not just one community resource. But all of these together.

If long-term residential recovery—like a state hospital rehab—is what is available and appropriate for an addict, as a community we can help provide resources for the family members at home. We know how to care for people when someone has a need. We have apps like Meal Train to schedule meals for people after surgery. We send the deacons to mow the lawn. We babysit kids when their mom is going through chemo. In the same way, we can care for families while Mom or Dad is in rehab.

We can also help the family members at home find ongoing resources that will help them. A recovery program, family counseling, maybe they're going to need a Habitat house built. The possibilities for caring for families in recovery are endless.

This is the new wave of recovery programs coming to us. The recovery management movement, launched by addiction professionals with decades of experience, shifts the focus of addiction treatment from *"acute stabilization* of people in crisis to a model focused on *sustaining* recovery."[4] Sustained recovery, according to William White, a long-respected recovery specialist, "forges a long-term partnership with patients, their families, and community support systems."[5]

The trouble with a show like *Intervention* is that it doesn't show the after. When or if your loved one goes into rehab, take a minute to celebrate that victory. But get ready to work just as hard to educate, stabilize, and prepare for reentry. Sustained recovery is all about a supportive and compassionate community.

ten

The Safety Net
of Social Services

> Bearing God's image establishes for every person a fundamental dignity which cannot be undermined either by wrongdoing or neediness.
>
> CHRISTINE POHL

The explosion of addiction in the United States has placed a heavy burden on an already strained social services system. The cost of the opioid epidemic was estimated in 2015 to be $504 billion a year, the bulk of which is borne by states and social services programs.[1] Because of the side effects of addiction, including job loss, family breakdown, health issues, legal battles, and homelessness, the need for housing assistance, food assistance, income assistance, and custodial care has increased dramatically. One-third of the half-million children in foster care are there because a parent is in active addiction.[2] And that number only takes into account cases in which addiction issues were recorded as the primary reason for parents losing custody.

For most of us, "social services" is an unknown entity and we lump all of government assistance together under the title "welfare." According to the Census Bureau, one-fifth of all Americans, including children, are on some form of assistance at any one time.[3] But the assistance for most people who use social services help is temporary. In the Temporary Assistance to Needy Families (TANF) program, which is only one part of social services and what we might call a "welfare check," participants receive assistance for less than a year. Many for only a month. And half of the participants in social services programs are single moms.

To someone who has not had to turn to them for help, social services may seem like a place where anyone can get a handout, but even with flaws, these programs provide a much-needed boost for people who might otherwise be homeless, go hungry, or be without medical care. Government assistance is not the lap of luxury it's sometimes made out to be. It's supposed to be a safety net for people who experience crisis in our affluent society. Yes, there are people who somehow work the system, but for families like ours, public assistance in our own crisis helped us feed our family while we struggled to get back on our feet with new jobs and a place to live.

The Nuances of Eligibility

I realize that for Christians, especially, there is a stigma attached to social services. To some it may be shocking to admit in print that we used social services, but for fifteen years family came to our aid when we were desperate. Through Dave's first rehab and a few relapses, we turned to them for help. Our families had helped us pick up the pieces, even paying off debts. But in 2007, as I assessed the complexity of our situation, I knew we would need ongoing help. Although I was grateful for every gift, I also felt tremendous shame. It wasn't like Dave was out of work because he was fighting cancer or got laid off. He had brought our troubles on himself. I felt I could not in good conscience go back to them again in 2007.

Of all the times in a person's life when you would think they would qualify for assistance for their family, job loss and homelessness would be right up at the top. However, there are holes in the system, and we found a lot of them. It turned out that this time Dave wasn't eligible for unemployment benefits. He'd been given the choice to resign or be fired. We thought "resign" on his employment record would give him a better chance of finding management work again. The truth of the situation was that Dave would not likely be hired in management for a very long time—not just in Christian ministries but in the general job market as well.

We'd only been at our church a couple of years. They didn't know us very well. And though they were willing to help with some of our needs, they had a process and limits at the time to their charitable giving. It seemed only right that I should exhaust whatever means I could find outside the church and our families. My search led me back to DSHS, the Department of Social and Health Services.

The Holes in the System

I think I cried more varieties of tears in November and December of 2007 than I've cried in my whole life combined. The joblessness, homelessness, Dave's relapse . . . painful sledgehammer blows to my pride. Shame and betrayal—still fresh—hung on my neck as I dragged myself into my meeting with a DSHS counselor.

As a family of six, our immediate physical needs were for food, jobs, a temporary place to live, medical insurance, and fuel for our huge gas-guzzling Suburban. Our secondary needs were first and last month's rent and deposit for renting a new place, another car with better gas mileage. (Gas was up over $4/gallon and the Suburban got 8 mpg; on a regular day, once Dave got a job, I traveled a minimum of fifty miles driving him and our kids around—$600 a month just for gas. These are hidden expenses we don't automatically recognize, and for which there are no benefits.) We also had regular bills to pay: the orthodontist, phone, college loans.

I brought it all with me: the last few pay stubs, severance letter, the kids' social security numbers, our drivers' licenses, bills—all the requisite documents listed on the DSHS website. According to their online calculator, we could be eligible for a month of TANF. (TANF works a little differently in each state.)[4]

What I discovered was a crack in the system. We had nothing in the bank, no jobs, no home, four children, and didn't qualify for one penny of assistance because of the method of the state's determination of resources. Dave's final paycheck was a consolidation of the three remaining paychecks from mid-November through the end of the year in one check, which had been garnished in its entirety to repay a part of the debt he owed the ministry. Three months of gross pay on one check with a net pay of zero. Technically, he'd *earned* the income though he didn't receive it, and because he earned it, we were ineligible for all assistance.

We know compassionate people work for DSHS. I did not happen to get one of them that day. "It doesn't matter that you didn't receive it," she said. "The government only cares that he earned it. Why did his employer garnish it?"

I told her about the drugs. I had to. And her response to me was, "If you leave him and get a legal separation, you would get assistance. That's what women in your situation usually do." She spoke without a shred of sympathy. "When you do that, you can reapply for TANF." And then she added, "You're lucky he's not in prison," in a way that told me she didn't really think I was "lucky." And now because I was afraid of the consequences of not having financial assistance, I wasn't so sure I was lucky myself.

As it stood, we could get no rental assistance, no cash benefit, and no food stamps for at least a month (due to the technicality with Dave's final paycheck), even though we had absolutely nothing. We were welcome to come back the next month and apply.

"But," she warned me, "everyone in the household over sixteen has to be pursuing full-time work in order to get anything more than food benefits."

I had no idea what all that meant, other than if I got a full-time job, our youngest would go to daycare. I tried to explain that, because I had a teaching credential, I could make more money working part-time as a teacher than working full-time doing anything else and then I wouldn't have to pay for daycare at all. But she said, "Full time. Those are the rules."

I stumbled out of that meeting into the bright fall air in a fog. All we needed was temporary help from DSHS. A couple of months, and then Dave and I would have paychecks. It seemed a cruel and unusual punishment to be forced into drastic choices this way. I wondered how many women in America who turn to DSHS for help opt to separate so they can actually get it for the sake of their children.

The Tie That Binds

An entry in *The Missionary Register for 1820* recounts the horror of the barbaric custom of *suttee*, burying or burning a living wife along with her dead husband.[5] The missionary wrote that he'd observed several suttee ceremonies in India. One wife, he reported, sat upright, stoically, next to the deceased, while friends and relatives shoveled dirt over them and then trampled the earth over her. Another was not so willingly tied to her husband as the fire was lit by her son and the pyre set adrift on the river. *The Register*, in publishing the incident, called on British women to be moved with compassion, coaxing them to come to India to teach women their value, that they were of more value alive than dead, that their fate was not tied to their dead husband, and that they were beloved by God as individuals apart from their husbands.

Although we don't observe this barbaric custom in the modern world, in America two hundred years later, we tie people to their spouse's fate. Not by the church, necessarily, but the state. The state in which I live, Washington, for example, is a mutual property state, which means your spouse's debts are your debts. In the year of our Lord 2019, you are just as responsible for them as he is—even if you don't know about them. Whether you live in a mutual property or common law state, research what your financial obligations could be so you are not blindsided.

Socioeconomic damage is a side effect of addiction that stays with you for a long, long time. No matter how repentant, how healthy, how back on track you are, this area of recovery is demoralizing. If addiction resulted in a job loss, it can be difficult to find another job. Debt collection calls go on and on for years.

This season of our lives was riddled with cruel irony. We experienced what so many would discover when the recession hit the following year: Dave's education and experience were a strike against him in the job market. He might as well have chosen to be fired for cause. In calls and interviews, prospective employers told Dave he was overqualified and a "hire risk" because employees with his résumé would leave as soon as they found a better job. "Why would you want to work for us?"

"Well," he'd say, "regular hours, proximity to home, health insurance . . ." And they'd ask, "Well, why not a job in the church? That's where your experience is . . ."

And conversations ended there. Dave was disqualified for ministry because of his addiction. At least until he had years of sobriety.

Digging Out of Poverty

This is the point of the story when people would probably leave their community. It's not worth the pain to stay put and rebuild their lives. So they pick up stakes and move far away and start over where no one knows them or their story or addictions. But we couldn't go. I believed if we did, we'd go back to keeping secrets and all of this nightmare would happen again. We needed to stay and rebuild where people knew us, all the worst of us, where I could let go of the debilitating stress of trying to hold Dave accountable because he had others invested in his daily life. This community, where we'd fallen flat on our faces, would be the lifeline for our marriage, our family, and our future.

So we sold our belongings and moved the rest into storage, a friend took our cat, and the six of us moved into Dave's parents' two-bedroom apartment with them. In the end, we never did receive TANF. Once we could report a full month of zero income, we qualified for food stamps. Dave's first paycheck from his new job, a third of his previous salary, and our eligibility for food stamps came at the same time, for which we were extremely grateful. Eventually, our church and our families helped us get into our own place.

I took an entry-level job in a marketing agency making barely above minimum wage. But the flexible hours meant I didn't have to spend my paycheck on childcare. Through a friend, we found a tiny townhouse to rent, located where I could walk to the store or to work if I needed to. But every pay increase, no matter how small, reduced our assistance—even though we were living well below the federal poverty level for more than a year. We struggled to put gas in our cars, and with the cost of gas hovering around $4 a gallon, sometimes I had to choose between eating dinner and driving all the kids to their schools.

DSHS benefits were a paperwork game every month. Managing our check-ins and keeping track of medical insurance updates was a big job that had to be done during work hours. I'd spend an hour on hold sometimes, only to give up because I had to go back to work. Government benefits also require regular updates like getting a signed form from a landlord. By the time our paperwork was processed, we'd lose more benefits, sometimes because of a twenty-five-cent raise. By the end of that year, my income went from $600 a month to $1200 a month and our food stamps went from $600 a month to nothing. Every raise zeroed out by loss of assistance. And one day our assistance stopped altogether.

In one way, this was good, because it meant we were getting back on our feet, but I could not help wondering, as we subsequently lost free lunch for our kids, *What is the point? What incentive is there for people to work hard and get out of poverty, if every step forward sends them back into financial insecurity?*

Lingering Side Effects of Addiction

In the middle of all this struggle to rebuild financially, we received a statement we'd been anticipating with anxiety for five months—Dave's remaining debts. When I opened the bill for several thousand dollars, I was sick. They wanted us to set up a payment plan. We were struggling to feed our family, there wasn't a dollar we could give. We were on the brink of summer. Four kids in childcare? There was no way we could manage that. Included with the statement was a contract requiring me to cosign for Dave's debt. The injustice of having to be responsible for Dave's debts sent me over the edge into anger and depression. Yes, I was lucky that they hadn't pressed charges against Dave. But I couldn't reconcile the heartache of being counted as co-conspirator. The blow struck deep.

I had done everything on the virtuous wife list—or the poor woman's version of it. At that point I wished I could cash in my virtue card for actual rubies, so I could sell them and buy gas for my car and pay childcare expenses, so I could get a better job. So much for the stay-at-home mom jewel in my crown. And the homeschool mom jewel. And the life-in-full-time-ministry jewel. It turned out there was no real earthly value in holding your marriage together. In the eyes of God and these witnesses, I was responsible *for* my husband, not just *to* him. The state does not respect healthy boundaries.

I was, along with our children, for all practical purposes, buried with Dave. And it would be a long, slow crawl out of that grave.

The Call to Restore Dignity

When we leave tangible acts of love and hospitality to institutions, rather than giving to the people in our lives, we depersonalize compassion. When we work together and come alongside struggling people, we not only give them the immediate help they need, but when we do it with a spirit of love and a commitment to restore dignity, we become instruments of change in their lives.

I wish we could all see caring for the poor and wandering among us as our God-given responsibility, but we don't. Instead we draw lines in the sand and redefine "neighbor" to suit us. There are plenty of stories of abusing the system that can make you cynical in a heartbeat. And then there are those for whom the system sort of works—like us. But the truth is, there are more people than we can possibly know who slip through the cracks of our social services system.

I remember one friend in crisis telling me she needed to feel like a real friend instead of feeling like a project. I understand this. As humiliating as DSHS was, at least I wasn't afraid they would take a picture of me applying for benefits that would show up in a Sunday slideshow. The biblical approach to community-based care gives people dignity. The people of Israel left portions of harvest in their fields to be gleaned by those who couldn't afford their own field. There were community meals, regular debt forgiveness, generational housing. These are all systems intended to help struggling people and they're still practiced in other parts of the world. But the distance between poverty and "self-sufficiency" is a no-man's-land in the United States. It's two steps forward, three back. And there are more enticing reasons to hang on to the help when you can get it than to kill yourself to stand on your own two feet.

Community was meant to stand in the gap, preventing homelessness, feeding those in need. Among the many verses in Scripture about caring for those in need, the apostle John says, "If anyone has material possessions and sees a brother or sister in need but has no pity on them, how can the love of God be in that person?"[6] Social services is not a place to find mercy. It's a help. Government can't base their DSHS requirements on mercy; they have formulas to help determine need. There is a place and a need for family and church and friends to come alongside those in crisis.

I cannot forget being poor. . . . I remember skipping recovery group one Friday night because we could not afford to buy gas or contribute to childcare. I sat on the landing between the flights of stairs of our tiny two-story townhouse, planning cheap meals to maximize food benefits and make them last the full month, praying for raises and hand-me-downs, and feeling ashamed of my ignorance and judgment of people in this affluent country who ask for help. I talked to God about how I would not forget my American poverty and would speak up and do something about it.

I'll be honest with you, it's pretty daunting. That past is painful. It's easy to take for granted simple things I do now, like buying a coffee at Starbucks or ignoring the cents ticking away on the gas pump or running into the grocery store for toilet paper and milk without the worry of overdrawing our bank account. It's been seven years, I think, since I last scrounged the floors of my car in search of change to literally buy bread. Being poor is time-consuming, stressful, and a sure trigger for relapse into addiction. *But for the grace of God*, we say. And I wonder if we really understand what that means.

eleven

Advocacy for Medical Care

Pain insists upon being attended to.

C. S. Lewis

A history of drug addiction complicates health care for people in recovery. Ordinary medical procedures suddenly become risks for relapse. Tracey Helton Mitchell was addicted to heroin and living on the streets of San Francisco when she was featured in an HBO documentary about black tar heroin addiction. Now clean and sober, and a recovery professional, she writes about what it was like to go into the hospital in the middle of a miscarriage as a person in recovery from opioid abuse:

> Before they put me under, I told my nurse I was an addict. He poked around my arms looking for a vein.
>
> "Those veins are gone," I assured him.
>
> He pulled my arm up to search the other side. Suddenly my mind clued in that they were going to inject me with drugs. I had not even taken a pain pill when I had a tooth extracted! Now, they

were about to shoot me up. Just like old times. For that split second, I was anticipating the deliciousness of drugs. Then I remembered why I was here: my baby. When the needle slipped into my skin, I felt the sting. What stung more was the fact that I really wanted to get high for the first time in many years. The loss of my baby was too much to bear. I had never been in this place before and it was ugly. I needed to ask for help.

I begged the nurse, "Please tell them I am in recovery."

He told me to relax as I felt the drugs go in. That was the last thing I remember for a few hours. When I snapped out of my drug haze, it was time to go home. I was shaky as I heard them explaining the post-operative instructions to Christian [her husband].

"Thirty Vicodin," I heard from the doctor.

"No. I can't," I whispered to Christian.

They were about to send me home from the hospital with thirty pills. I wanted to die, and they were giving me the means to kill myself.[1]

Tracey's experience is heartbreaking—even more so because a prescription for pain pills after an outpatient surgery was how she got into addiction in the first place. The entire experience could have sent her spiraling back into addiction or left her dead from an overdose. By this point in her life, Tracey was already a recovery professional and knew she had to make a plan for how to manage the pain medication she needed that involved someone else holding on to her medication and dispensing the pills. "I was not going to set myself up for failure," she says. Others, like Jessie Grubb, have not been so fortunate.

Jessie's hospital story made headlines because a year before she died, her family met President Obama at a Town Hall meeting about the opioid crisis. After several stints in rehab, Jessie, just thirty years old, went into the hospital for surgery. Doctors didn't know she was a recovering drug addict, and they prescribed opioids when she left the hospital. She died the next day from an overdose.

Doctors' Office Dangers

Imagine going to the hospital for care, and the drug you know will cause you to relapse is not only offered but pushed on you. For patients who've battled addiction to any form of drug, doctors' offices, emergency rooms, and hospitals are formidable and cause stress that those of us who have not abused drugs can't understand. Medical personnel, especially in emergency rooms, have to rely on their best judgment. They don't always have a person's medical records available before treatment, and patients don't always have advocates. In 2017, Jessie's Law was introduced to the Senate:

> Sec. 2) This bill requires the Department of Health and Human Services (HHS) to develop and disseminate best practices for health care providers and state agencies regarding the display of a patient's history of opioid addiction in the patient's medical records.[2]

And in 2018, government and medical officials met to brainstorm details for chart notifications for patients in recovery.

—⊣{ DAVE —

It used to be that the only way you could get a serious red flag on your chart that would alert doctors with a big sign—a large laminated red card on your door so the doctor couldn't miss it—was to say you had a life-threatening allergy. At my doctor's office, the medical staff knew that I was in recovery, but when I ended up in the hospital a few years ago with a gall bladder attack, we had to explain all over again. When the intern asked incredulously, "So you're allergic to painkillers?" Deb snort-laughed, and I said, "No, I'm in recovery." And we got the response we've been used to hearing for years: "Wow, you don't look like an addict." By now, when statistics show that one in five people prescribed opioids misuse them, you would think the shock would be worn off.[3] "Not looking like an addict" is how I was able to doctor shop for years without raising alarm.

—⊣}——

Many of us mistakenly think dangerously addictive drugs are too highly regulated for an honest person to become an addict, but that simply isn't true. It's disturbing how often opioids are prescribed—a teen for wisdom teeth extraction, a child for a cough. And we take them. Blindly trusting that the doctor knows best. We're sent home after minor surgical procedures with major prescriptions even when all we really need is ibuprofen and rest.

Opioids are a normal part of our American lives now. Chances are, you or your children have taken opioids for big things like surgery recovery and for lesser procedures like oral surgery, for coughs, and even for nausea. According to the National Institute on Drug Abuse, all opioids have a high potential for abuse. And some drugs aren't classified as opioid but were designed to act just like an opioid on the brain. Obviously not everyone who takes painkillers becomes addicted to them. But those with a family history of addiction or who suffer from chronic pain or a serious injury, taking medications for long periods of time, are vulnerable.

"High school students who are prescribed opioids have a 33 percent increased risk of later misusing the drugs."[4] This is where trouble starts for many who become addicted to drugs. The potential for addiction is so great in the thirteen-to-thirty age window, some states now have a three-day limit on post–dental procedure prescriptions. Young adults get their first taste of a high after getting their wisdom teeth out or after surgery, as in Tracey Helton Mitchell's experience. Because additional studies have shown regular NSAIDs like ibuprofen are more effective for post–oral surgery pain management, the American Medical Association is now calling on oral surgeons to prescribe NSAIDs instead of the standard hydrocodone, which is an opioid.[5]

Early in Dave's recovery he needed oral surgery. When we talked over our concerns with the surgeon, he said Dave really didn't need to take heavy-duty painkillers; Tylenol and ibuprofen would work just fine. "For this sort of oral surgery (tooth extraction) we give painkillers for comfort, but he'll be fine without them and it's not worth the risk."

Depersonalized Care

The trouble is, we don't have time for pain and we don't give ourselves time to heal. This drive to keep going has created the perfect environment for dependency on pills to grow. Our hurry-up culture has affected the entire business of medicine. When we're sick, we feel the pressure to get well, get back to work, and earn that paycheck. The push to be well before we actually are increases dependency on drugs to help us function.

Care has been depersonalized and our doctors don't know us. It's wonderful to be able to run into an urgent care for a cough that's keeping our baby up all night, for stitches when we cut a finger, an X-ray and casting a broken arm. But we're in and out of surgery now too. The speedy-care model has replaced relationship in our generation. Now we demand it. Urgent care, insurance changes, and restructuring of medical groups have made it nearly impossible to hang on to the same primary care doctor year after year.

A doctor who has spent only a few minutes with you cannot diagnose whether you have "an addictive personality" or "fit the profile of an addict." We have to monitor ourselves. I've heard doctors and dentists say to someone in recovery, "Oh, it's just for a few days. A small dose won't hurt." Or "Five years clean is plenty. You'll be fine taking it for a few days." Time alone does not make a person in recovery safe from relapse. It doesn't matter how many years clean they are.

Through the years of dealing with Dave's addiction to pain medication and now years of his recovery, we've learned the hard way that we can't always rely on medical staff to make the right decisions for us. A part of my blindness to what I realized later were very obvious signs of an addiction problem was that doctors kept prescribing Tramadol to Dave. It was not until 2014 that Tramadol even became a scheduled drug. When I called doctors' offices in 2004 to talk about bills, I told them Dave was addicted to Tramadol. Doctors called back to defend their prescriptions. To this day, it's a fight to get medical personnel to understand Tramadol is addictive. Ortho-McNeil pharmaceuticals did such a masterful job of marketing their drug as safe, it's become the go-to alternative painkiller in hospitals across the country.

Lack of Addiction Training

Medical professionals need more training on how to handle prescription opioids, narcotics, and recovering addicts. The National Center on Addiction and Substance Abuse at Columbia University released a report on addiction medicine that revealed medical students only receive a few hours of training regarding addiction.[6] This leaves doctors at the mercy of pharmaceutical drug reps who bring bags of samples and buy meals for the office staff and give very little training on the meds patients ask for. Add to that the pressure we put on doctors to keep us from feeling pain and discomfort, to get us in and out of their offices quickly and back to work as fast as possible, and we've got a cultural landscape that is ripe for addiction.

Overprescribing Drugs

As consumers, we need to educate ourselves instead of relying on physicians to always make the right decision for us. The American Dental Association, in response to research relating teenagers' oral surgery prescriptions to future addiction, says you don't have to prescribe such heavy medication.[7] Especially for young people. They are resilient. If a woman can have a baby without meds, a healthy seventeen-year-old athlete can certainly recover from tooth extraction without a week on pain pills. Is it really necessary to give a twelve-year-old a narcotic for a broken finger?

I don't trust medical providers who jump to drugs anymore. When my son was on a gurney with a fractured bone attempting to escape his skin, pain medication was the first thing I asked for—well, demanded. The reason for his pain was obvious. But when the first response to a headache, a stomachache, or a pain in the ribs is "Take this narcotic and call your primary care physician on Monday," it's disconcerting.

But how can we measure a loved one's pain? If medical professionals can't tell, how are you as an uneducated layman supposed to be able to tell? Where does a patient taking medication prescribed by a doctor cross the lines from use to dependence to addiction? Opiates and narcotics are difficult to stop taking. Withdrawal—even after a few days—can make you feel sick. And withdrawal after years on these powerful medications can kill you.[8] Ask doctors for other relief options before giving yourself or your child an opioid. There are alternatives, especially for coughs and dental procedures. And dispose of all pain medications wisely. Do not keep them around for the next time you have pain.

The good news is, because of the crisis, some hospitals are implementing new surgical procedures that reduce the need for serious painkillers after surgery. In addition, rules for dentists and oral surgeons are restricting the amount of pills they can prescribe. These innovative approaches are expected to help prevent addiction.

Complications in Care

People in recovery face additional complications that affect access to medical care.

Fear of going to the doctor. Just being in a doctor's office can be stressful and trigger anxiety or craving for someone recovering from prescription drug addiction of any kind. If the doctor's office was where they sought a fix, it's like an alcoholic walking into his former favorite bar.

Being banned from doctors' offices. Doctor shopping gets prescription drug addicts—and even their families—into trouble. When Dave was still struggling with addiction, we received certified letters from doctors' offices informing us that they would "no longer treat you or your family members." Because of this, it was years before we could access services at the biggest medical group in our town, including the only local OB-GYN covered by our insurance.

Complications with insurance. Medical debts can be a hinderance to people in recovery receiving the care they need. It was for us. We are fortunate that Washington State has a health care system that provides low-cost medical insurance for all kids. Not every family has that safety net. In addition, most health care plans do not include long-term care for recovery. Thirty days is the usual coverage.

Dismissive medical staff. It's important for someone in recovery to find a medical provider who understands the side effects of addiction and how they can linger into recovery. Long-term drug abuse can do significant damage to the liver and kidneys. Even after more than a decade clean, Dave's doctor still checks these regularly. But it's more than that—you need a doctor who understands how critical it is for you to stay away from drugs that could trigger a relapse. If your doctor doesn't understand this, find another one. If they're dismissive or if they minimize your concerns, it's a good sign that they're not going to be supportive. Dismissiveness is the worst response a medical professional can have for opioid addiction recovery. We've had to fight for Dave's sobriety in medical situations. It's frustrating and it's disheartening.

The Role of an Advocate

Family members can be important advocates for their loved one in recovery, especially when they are able to manage it with grace and respect. For the last decade, Dave has invited me into at least the initial appointment with a doctor. He explains why I'm there. Sometimes doctors are understanding, sometimes they look at me with skepticism, but for us it's worth the awkward minutes. Someday, maybe advocacy for patients in recovery from opioid addiction will become standard practice.

We don't intend for this advice to apply to terminal patients. And though Dave's addiction began with chronic pain, chronic pain management is also a separate issue. Though it's important to be wise about medication, dependence and addiction are not the same thing. However, the side effects of long-term medicating make it worth investigating alternative therapies.

We are so grateful that Dave has had only a few migraines since getting off drugs. We will never know how many of hundreds of headaches were side effects of drug abuse and whether the pills were actually feeding his pain.

Plan for Pain

Ask anyone in recovery from painkiller addiction what their greatest fear is and they will tell you it's pain. Pain from an injury, pain from a dental procedure, pain from surgery. At these moments, pain medications will be offered freely, often medications they've abused or were addicted to. The potential for destroying their sobriety with a prescription cannot be underestimated. One of the most critical facets of recovery from pill addiction is an understanding of how to deal with pain in the future. Having a pain management plan in place can prevent relapse and save the life of a patient in recovery from drug addiction.

The worst time to make a decision about pain management is when you are in post-op coming out of anesthesia. Dave ran into a similar situation as Tracey Helton Mitchell and Jessie Grubb did when he had gall bladder surgery a few years ago. Fortunately, this surgery was planned, which gave him the opportunity to discuss postoperative pain management with his surgeon. Even with this plan in place, however, we ran into some stressful moments and arguments with medical personnel in the hospital.

Meeting the Medical Team

I accompanied Dave to the surgeon for his pre-op visit, to the hospital, and into postoperative recovery. Even though we'd set up a pain management plan beforehand, including talking with the anesthesiologist, nursing staff, and surgeon, because the hospital's standard procedure with outpatient surgery was to send the patient home with pain pills, the first thing the nurse said to me post-op was, "So we're going to send him home with a prescription for painkillers." I said *no way*, of course, and Dave, in his anesthesia stupor refused to take anything at all. But our surgeon said denying pain management completely can put a patient in a very bad place if their pain gets out of control, because it will take more medication to get them back to a reasonable level of pain. Which is exactly what you don't want.

We had a good deal of discussion, including reiterating to the nurse that Tramadol, the hospital's painkiller of choice, was actually very bad for Dave because he had been addicted to it in the past. Even though he'd been clean for almost a decade at that point, we had no desire to test his recovery. We waited for our surgeon to come out of surgery and went through the entire plan again. "We want to avoid—at all costs—sending him home with a bottle of pills," Dave's surgeon said to me at one point, "even if it means we have to keep him overnight."

In the end, Dave was admitted to the hospital for an overnight stay so they could manage his pain intravenously, without resorting to pain pills. Because Dave's surgeon recommended it, he got it. He was the most important person to have on our side, because he was the final word to the rest of the team.

Be Prepared to Be a Problem

Unfortunately, we still weren't out of the woods, because the specifics didn't get into his orders. Three separate times during Dave's stay, at every shift change, I had to advocate for him to remain on IV meds and not be given Tramadol pills. Each time I had to explain his addiction. Each time the nurse was skeptical because "Tramadol is not addictive." I had to push until Dave came around enough to advocate for himself.

Dave received pain medication through an IV during and after surgery for about twenty-four hours total. They used just enough to cut the pain quickly to give the slower-acting—but very effective—IV a chance to work. I was grateful for that. Staying was definitely the best choice. In Tracey Helton Mitchell's case, as she had been an IV drug user, her postoperative pain management plan involved pills instead of an IV. She was sent home to recover, and an advocate held her pain pills and dispensed them, rather than leaving the pills with her so she could medicate herself. This was critical because she was in so much anguish over the loss of her baby. Precautions like these help keep former addicts from overdose.

When Someone Else in Your House Is on Pain Medication

A few years before Dave's surgery, I had gall bladder surgery too, and my own recovery was extremely stressful just because of the presence of pain medications. Dave was only four years clean from pills, and I did not want to set temptation in front of him. I made sure to get the medication I needed before my surgery so that Dave didn't have to pick up the prescription. I hid the pills and counted them for my own peace of mind. I weaned myself off them as quickly as possible. Since then, a few of our kids and our pets have had major medical procedures, and our management plan is always the same. I fill the prescriptions, I hold them, I dispense

A Word about Medically Assisted Detox

—H DAVE—

Some people in addiction recovery are going through medically assisted detox. Drugs like buprenorphine (Suboxone) are used for some patients to manage opioid dependence. In just two pills, Suboxone gave me the sense of well-being that I'd gotten from thirty Tramadol. For some people, this method seems to work. It did not work for me. As soon as I ran out of it, I went back to taking Tramadol. In theory, Suboxone is another wonder drug, intended to help people with chemical addiction work toward freedom from that addiction. But addiction isn't just physical and mental—it's multifaceted. Which is why, for Suboxone to be effective, the patient must find ethical, trained professionals and has to be committed to the full course of treatment—meetings, counseling, and all.

However, Suboxone did help me in my final withdrawal from Tramadol and made the physical withdrawal process more bearable. I did not have to be hospitalized. I had to taper off the Suboxone, which took me down to tiny pieces of the pill—milligrams. The detox was difficult and emotional. I didn't begin to feel normal until several months after my last piece of pill. It wasn't easy, but it was possible. I got clean!

them, and I dispose of them. Dave's sobriety is entirely worth the hassle. There's been no reason for us to take a chance.

When Advocacy Is Unwelcome

Dave's openness about his addiction and recovery has been a lifesaver. We were able to tell our employers *why* when we ask for time off for recovery from surgery. Dave had and has a job that not only allows him time to heal, but they prayed over him specifically that the drugs he needed for his surgery would not be a trigger for him to relapse. And we've found a primary care office where everyone understands, where our children can say they have a family history of addiction, and now no one blinks an eye. It's a supportive medical community. But we had to initiate and work for it.

Of course, you can't force your loved one into a plan for postoperative care. Patient privacy laws mean anyone over sixteen is responsible for themselves. You can encourage them to request a plan. You can ask if you can be part of it. In this process, it's so important not to shame them. Your loved one may only be comfortable giving you permission if they trust you. The more dignity you give them at home, the more likely they'll invite you to be their advocate or respond positively when you ask. Advocacy is not punishment. You're supposed to be on their side, *for* their recovery. Ask if your presence would be helpful. A parent's presence doesn't always ease stress levels.

Sponsors can be good advocates too. If your loved one in recovery is facing surgery, gently approach working on a plan together. If they don't want you to be a part of it, or if they don't live with you, encourage them to have their sponsor or trusted friend take on that role.

We can take all the precautions in the world, but in the end, we ultimately have to trust God with our loved one.

Recovery from opioid addiction complicates medical issues. It's uncomfortable. It's inconvenient. It may require our time and sacrifice. We may even have to address our control issues or our recovering loved one's lack of trust in us. We may have failed them in the past. We may need to forgive ourselves and ask their forgiveness. We may get into uncomfortable conversations with other family members about the meds they have in their house. Sobriety is so worth defending.

Let gentleness be your guide. Strive for healing. Your respectful advocacy could spark change that transforms a community.

twelve

A Restorer of Homes

> Compassionate love is the axis of the Christian moral revolution and the only sign ever given by Jesus by which a disciple would be recognized.
>
> BRENNAN MANNING

Compassion isn't a formula or step. It's not convenient, or Instagram-worthy, or instantly gratifying. Compassion costs us. Somewhere between *bear one another's burdens* and *each one shall bear his own load* is a no-man's-land. This desolate space has become the domain of relationship experts and guides. We cling to maps and formulas, but it doesn't take long before we realize there's no perfect system. No flowchart guarantees the outcomes we desire.

At some point, we have to shut out the voices, set aside ourselves, and listen to what Jesus is trying to say to us, in the moment, about the person right in front of us.

Cross Bearing

For many of us, there is no greater death to self than adding your burden to mine. This, *this* is the place of Jesus. Jesus who bore our own sins on the tree but who also asks us to daily pick up our cross and follow him. What will happen if we take seriously the call of Jesus to come and die to ourselves?[1]

When I consider the implications of picking up a cross daily, I wonder, have we—in the name of *best lives* and *boundaries* and *tough love*—forgotten the power of laying down our lives for our friends? What could laying down our lives involve other than entering spaces that will mean forsaking our own needs, our own comfort, and maybe a heap of common sense? There is nothing commonsensical about choosing to make our life more complicated. And complication is what we get when we take the step into the hard-to-define spaces of where my responsibilities end and yours begin. It's what we get when we pick up the cross—a cross not of our own making, but of someone else's, unjustly laid on us, just as Jesus's cross was unjustly laid on him.

Maybe in the past you've been successful at keeping your distance from this place where common sense, science, psychology, theories, and theology collide. But chances are, if you picked up this book, you are torn between your head and your heart in some way. Because of addiction, someone in your life has moved cross bearing from theory to practice. This is someone you care about, someone you love.

We may never win the War on Drugs in the way we wish we could. But that shouldn't stop us from fighting the battle in front of us the best way we can: one person at a time, starting with the person in addiction recovery in our own lives. This opioid epidemic is powerful, and we need to lay down our own agenda, our own timeline, and pray to be bold and have courage and strength. And even more critical: compassion. A heart moved by a deep love that *believes all things, hopes all things, bears all things,* and *endures* is not easily made. Unfailing love is not doable in our own strength. It is the mark of Christ on our life. The crisis may not kill us, but it may require us to die to ourselves.

Living Proof

The resurrection of Lazarus enraged the chief priests. From that moment on, they made plans to kill him—because Lazarus was powerful living evidence that Jesus was exactly and undeniably who he claimed to be. "On account of him many of the Jews were deserting them and believing in Jesus," the apostle John wrote.[2] According to some early church traditions, Lazarus's friends ended up having to physically protect him from the religious leaders who tried to have him killed. Word spread quickly. Within days a huge crowd had gathered to welcome Jesus into Jerusalem—the week before they crucified him. The resurrection of Lazarus, whose name means "whom God helps," leads us right to the cross.

There is a spiritual and physical application here for the community around a recovering addict. "All human nature vigorously resists grace," wrote Flannery O'Connor, "because grace changes us and the change is painful."[3] There are graceless, merciless people who cannot understand forgiveness and love. Those who do not believe God is powerful enough to transform even the worst sinner, let alone a prescription drug addict. They would have addicts in recovery dragged into the marketplace, flogged, spit on, mocked, purely to satisfy their vindictive spirit. And they may not stop there. They may attack spouses, children, friends, the church—anyone who accepts your healing—because tearing them down isn't enough. It galls them to see addicts loved and forgiven.

I am in no way a model of perfect faith. I've done my fair share of forcing my agenda, I've hurled plenty of pots at Dave along with a few *curse God and die*s.[4] But as much as Dave's healing proves addiction doesn't have to end in death, *together* we are proof that it doesn't have to end a marriage either. And right there, in that sentence, is what took me so long to get this book out into the world. It's scary to put that on the page, print, bind, and distribute it. It's like a perfectly packaged invitation to attack.

This book, in your hands, is a triumph over fear that this truth will be tested more than it already has been. With it comes a plea for prayer for every Lazarus man, woman, and marriage are proof of God's healing and sacrificial love. I can tell you that as exciting as resurrection is, it's also terrifying, because letting you exist as living proof of a God who heals is not on the enemy's game plan. So I ask you to pray. For your own marriage or child or friend or neighbor. For yourself. And for Dave and me and ours. ("Let anyone who thinks that he stands take heed lest he fall."[5]) Two thousand years later, we've still got Pharisees, secular and religious, and sometimes the enemy is us.

Dave's journey through pain management, dependence, addiction, and intensive recovery ran through twenty of our nearly twenty-seven years of life together so far. There is no part of our lives the poison of addiction did not touch. But the last eleven years have been a testament to the grace of God. We've been reworked, reformed—each of us, separately and together. In some ways, the change has been so profound that when we look back, we don't recognize our old selves.

Sometimes when I read my volumes of journals, it doesn't even seem like the man I was writing about then is the man I live with today. God has really changed him—and me. He's transformed us.

A Decade of Healing

I'm wrapping up writing this book a few weeks before Christmas. A few days ago, our daughter got home from a semester in England. A few hours ago, one of our boys arrived from Idaho. And in a few more, Dave will be home with our third college student who's been in school in California. Our youngest, a junior in high school now, has another week of school before the break.

I'm grateful for the decade of healing we've had and that the sadness and despair of addiction and early years of uncertainty in recovery are long past. There is a joy in our family that has grown through some hard, hard years, with the help of transparency and love. For better or worse, we aren't into secrets.

Christmas has another layer of beauty for us.

The date today, December 14, is a big one. On this day, exactly eleven years ago, Dave took his last pill. I rifled through my boxes of journals to find the one that is almost entirely just the six miserable weeks of our lives after Dave was let go from his job and we faced homelessness and poverty.

On that day, I read these words by Henri Nouwen and copied them into my journal:

> You have to move gradually from crying outward—crying out for people who you think can fulfill your needs—to crying inward to the place where you can be held and carried by God, who has become incarnate in the humanity of those who love you in community. No one person can fulfill all your needs. But the community can truly hold you. The community can let you experience the fact that, beyond your anguish, there are human hands that hold you and show you God's faithful love.[6]

I flipped the page back to the day before. . . . I stood on the porch of our house at the camp while a sheriff questioned me about the 911 call I'd placed on our house phone before abruptly hanging up. Dave and I had had a fight. A bad one. He was at the end of tapering off Suboxone, and I was an absolute emotional wreck. We fought because he wanted me to tell him how he could fix things in the wake of losing everything. He threatened suicide, and I threatened to call the police. He tried to hold me back from the phone, and I kicked him hard. We were jolted to our senses and both cooled off the instant the 911 operator called back. They had traced the call to the camp and a sheriff was driving around, asking staff and guests which house was ours. Bringing the police into our fight, on the camp property, in the middle of a guest group staying there, even after all we'd been through, was a new low.

The Gift of Community

Embracing community meant letting people into our shame: our family, friends, our pastor and church, counselors, recovery groups, medical and social workers. It was hard and humbling to let human hands hold us. It required letting down walls. In the end, commitment to living in truth and letting people into our mess saved us.

We had to move from the camp the week after Christmas that year. As awful as it was for Dave and me, for our kids the entire situation was both devastating and scary. They had to leave a place they loved, a life at camp that had been more fun for them than any presents could be. Rather than receiving, they were losing. There was nothing we could do for them that would make up for this hurt. There wasn't even anything we could do for them for Christmas. Desperate for hope, we started writing on a poster board in our living room every blessing we received. It was a daily reminder to all of us during those depressing winter weeks that God still really did care about us. He was showing his love for us through people.

Everything we received during that time was a gift from someone. We had absolutely nothing, we earned nothing. Many of our friends and family and even the staff of our kids' schools helped us with food and paying our regular bills and our church helped us with rent. Still, we were deeply depressed and discouraged by our circumstances. Dave was deep in withdrawal, and I was hanging on by a thread.

I forget now where Dave's parents were that Christmas. Perhaps Brazil to visit Dave's sister. I think we were supposed to have gone to California to spend the holiday with my extended family, but our current crisis prevented that. At any rate, somehow we ended up being far away from family and alone at the camp for Christmas that year, scraping together some sort of celebration in our sad, packed-up house at the cold, empty camp. Our lovely tree—the nicest we'd ever had and which Dave's parents had gotten for us—was going to be rather lonely.

The kids remember details of that night better than I do. We'd gone out someplace, they say, maybe Christmas Eve service at our church, and we forgot to turn on the porch light. When we came home and pulled up to the house, the headlights illuminated a bunch of black garbage bags on our darkened front porch.

"Mom, you were so mad," the kids say. "You thought someone had put their trash on our porch!" They laugh about my fury and muttering. And that I would think someone would do something so mean to us on Christmas Eve. "But you went ahead of us, and when you got close to the pile of bags, you started crying and we didn't know why."

As we recount that night, that's when we all lose it. We all have tears, remembering the sight.

The bags were heavy—filled with presents. Some from friends, some from strangers.

The children's theater group we'd been a part of for a couple of years had already been so generous to us with gift cards and food. But now it seemed that they had done even more. There were several gifts from the director and her family and other families. And one of the girls from the theater, Lauren, who was in sixth grade at the time, had even gotten her class at school to buy Christmas presents for each of our kids. There were dozens of gifts! So much generosity—we were overwhelmed.

Christmas morning was absolutely delightful. There were so many surprises. So many sweet gifts. The list of presents fills fifty lines of my otherwise very sad journal. It was a Christmas we will never forget.

Instruments of Grace

I want to remember always the kind of compassion that was poured out on us. To not forget the help given to us by God, by our church, by family and friends. We had years of struggle ahead of us, but moments of kindness and compassion encouraged us and gave us hope that our pain and sadness would not last forever.

In those early months of recovery and poverty, I found a job writing for nonprofit ministries all over the country. As I interviewed and wrote up the stories of addicts and their families, I sat in my cubicle and sobbed silently, grateful for the padded walls between me and the rest of my creative team.

In the middle of that year, when there were days we couldn't afford gas for the car, I interviewed the president of a rescue mission over the phone. He talked briefly about brokenness and the path to restoration. When he spoke these words from Isaiah to me, I know he had no idea what they meant to me or how they would seep into my soul.

"Spend yourselves on behalf of the hungry and satisfy the needs of the oppressed," he quoted from Isaiah. While he read the rest of chapter 58, tears ran down my face, and I prayed to God that someday Dave and I would become instruments of his grace in the lives of others going through the devastation of addiction. And that is our prayer for you.

At the heart of recovery is a compassionate community that dispenses grace along with tangible, practical help for those in trouble. God has restored our home through his mercy and the compassion of our community in ways Isaiah recorded centuries before Lazarus was raised from the dead. We are grateful for the last eleven years of sobriety, and we are grateful that our story of devastation and restoration can bring some hope to families and communities. This is God's plan for healing. We are, all of us, called to spend ourselves to restore our loved ones, our neighbors, our communities. And, in the end, it turns out, we've been restored ourselves.

> Share your food with the hungry,
> and give shelter to the homeless.

Give clothes to those who need them,
and do not hide from relatives who need your help.

Then your salvation will come like the dawn,
and your wounds will quickly heal.
Your godliness will lead you forward,
and the glory of the Lord will protect you from
behind.
Then when you call, the Lord will answer.
"Yes, I am here," he will quickly reply.

Remove the heavy yoke of oppression.
Stop pointing your finger and spreading vicious
rumors!
Feed the hungry,
and help those in trouble.
Then your light will shine out from the darkness,
and the darkness around you will be as bright as noon.
The Lord will guide you continually,
giving you water when you are dry
and restoring your strength.
You will be like a well-watered garden,
like an ever-flowing spring.
Some of you will rebuild the deserted ruins of your cities.
Then you will be known as a rebuilder of walls
and a restorer of homes.

Isaiah 58:7–12 NLT

Acknowledgments

Gratitude

Thank you to the team at Revell: Andrea Doering, for seeing the need for this book and for championing, cheering, and steering it (and me) to completion. Thank you, Barb Barnes, for your hard work and rework on the details of this book. We are so grateful for your personal investment in this project and for helping shape it. Thank you, Erin Smith, for your work marketing and spreading the word, and Patti Brinks, for your cover design.

Thanks to Mount Hermon Writers Conference for the "first timer" scholarship that led to meeting Andrea. To Emily Freeman and Elisa Pulliam for guidance in the author journey. And to Bill Jensen for your generosity and wisdom. And thank you to my critique partners: Anna, Emily, Maggie, and Jennica.

To the teams at Masterworks and A Brave New—I'm a better writer because of you and the ministries who let me share their mission with the world. Thank you especially to Burt Rosen at KARM, whose heart of hope (expressed in chap. 12) still encourages me.

Thank you to Salem Alliance for your Life Path program and partnership. To the ICADTS, the NACR, and all who study and serve to help people recover from addiction. I'm grateful to include your work in these pages.

Thank you to everyone who took the time to read this manuscript and to Sara Adams, Jane Teller, Tamara Rice, Mikal Kildal, and Jim Walter, who gave us invaluable feedback. And to the generous readers who endorsed this book, your words are a gift to us.

Thank you to my fellow hope*writer authors group for the lifeline you've been for this last year of writing. I can't imagine it without you.

And thank you, Mom, for your relentless encouragement to "write it all down" and Dad for your experience and encouragement in all the stages of writing. I'm so blessed to have grown up in a family that values creativity.

This book is a love letter to community that was and has been part of our story.

Thank you, Wayne and Laura Morris, who loved us and guided us and pastored us in ways we still feel and try to emulate today. Thank you to Lauren and the Gateway 6th grade class of '07–08, the staff and families of Pearson Elementary, KCMT, CSTOCK, Cornerstone, and Island Lake who caught us that Christmas. Anne, Denise, Tony, Meagan, Jeff—your words of love and encouragement and your arms around us still feel like grace.

Thank you to the Celebrate Recovery families at Bayside and Cornerstone. We hope you find yourselves in these pages.

Thank you, Mark and Sally Healy, Eric and Sheryl Rasmussen, and Dave and Cindy Lester, for making room for a family of six in your homes. We are still grateful for the welcome and sacrifice.

Thank you to the team at AFS for hiring a guy coming out of addiction and giving him dignity. Thank you, Restore Church and The Alliance Northwest, for welcoming Dave into full-time ministry.

Thank you to our Restore Church family! We love you. Thank you to Jim Walter for loving and leading us as our pastor and friend for the past fifteen years. To Tim Gates and Dave Damon and Jim for praying over us for healing and for a blessing on our work together. Thank you to our community group for your constant encouragement, prayers for boldness, and celebration: Trish, Chuck, Kevin, Renée, Ben, Darcy, Josh, and Kyla.

Thank you to our faithful blog readers, podcast listeners, subscribers, and friends who have helped us spread hope farther than we ever could have by ourselves. Thank you, Melinda Gray, for your unwavering enthusiasm across the miles. And thank you, Jim Hinch, for handing Dave and me a megaphone.

Bill and Barb Barrick, Darrell and Ruthanne Beddoe, thank you for being parents with open arms and loving hearts. You loved and prayed fervently for us for many years, you sheltered us, and provided for us time and again and we are grateful to pass the legacy of your love on to our children.

Thank you to our brothers and sisters: Tim and Danika Barrick for believing and rescuing. To Paul Beddoe and Ron Di Gregorio, Nate and Sandy Barrick, Sarah Beddoe, Anna and Caleb Simpson, and Nate and Tamara Rice. We are so grateful you supported us—over and over. We are grateful you are not only our siblings but our friends.

To our extended families far and near who have loved us, encouraged us, walked beside us in suffering and rejoiced with us in healing. I don't know if we'll ever fully know the extent of your goodness to us. Thank you, Aunt Nancy and Uncle John, for praying this book out into the world.

To Jane Teller and Kit Verhofstadt, my life models and soul sisters. I'm so grateful to you for your deep friendship and for leading the way in this journey of following Jesus. To Trish Silvernale for your love, laughter, and goodness to me and my family. And to Tamara Rice, my sister, writing partner, fellow dreamer, accomplished and wise editor, and my lifelong dearest friend. Oh, how I love you.

And to Dave, thank you is not enough. This book doesn't exist without your commitment to recovery and bringing good news for people who need hope. Thank you for not only allowing me to share your story but encouraging me to do it. Your contribution to this book is so much more than blocks of words and years blended in these pages. You've been a coach, an editor, sounding board, shopper, cook, and pet wrangler, and have held our household together in ways only people who live with authors understand. I love you.

Thank you to our children for enduring my forgetfulness, my astonishing dependence on tacos for your nutritional needs, and for being the absolute greatest cheerleaders a writer could ask for. I am always and ever overwhelmed by your words of affirmation. I love you, Katie, Calvin, George, and Henry. You are proof of God's grace and kindness to your dad and me.

Deborah Beddoe
Poulsbo, Washington
July 30, 2019

Appendix

Resources

A. Organizations

- National Association for Christian Recovery—nacr.org

  A wealth of information, resources, and encouragement for families and individuals in recovery.

- Celebrate Recovery—celebraterecovery.com

  Learn more about 12 Step groups for Christians, find a group, find help.

- Hazelden Betty Ford Foundation—hazeldenbettyford.org

  A comprehensive website for addiction and recovery resources.

- HHS Opioid Epidemic Practical Toolkit—https://www.hhs.gov/about/agencies/iea/partnerships/opioid-toolkit/index.html

  This fantastic website, a collaboration of faith-based and community nonprofits (including those mentioned above), provides resources, training, and practical information for churches, communities, and individuals. Even if your church does not have capacity for a recovery program, there's so much you can do to be a welcome place for people who are struggling. Find out more here.

B. Recommended Reading

A noncomprehensive list of books that we recommend.

Compassion

Abba's Child and *Ragamuffin Gospel* by Brennan Manning

What's So Amazing About Grace by Philip Yancey

Everybody's Normal Till You Get to Know Them by John Ortberg

Now I Lay My Isaac Down by Carol Kent

Understanding the 12 Steps from a Christian perspective

Spiritual Kindergarten: Christian Perspectives on the Twelve Steps by Dale and Juanita Ryan

A Hunger for Healing by J. Keith Miller

Life's Healing Choices by John Baker

Life Recovery Bible by Stephen Arterburn and David Stoop

Books for pastors/churches

The Recovery-Minded Church by Jonathan Benz

Bridges to Grace by Liz Swanson and Teresa McBean

Living into Community by Christine D. Pohl

Stepping Out: With Hope and Healing for a Hurting World by Jane Marjerrison Wolf

The Community of God by Douglas Bursch

Leaders who need help dealing with recovery themselves

Shattered Dreams: God's Unexpected Pathway to Joy by Larry Crabb

Leading with a Limp by Dan Allender

Spouses

Codependent No More and *Beyond Codependency* by Melody Beattie

The Dance of Anger by Harriet Lerner

The Gifts of Imperfection and *Daring Greatly* by Brené Brown

Because I Said Forever by Deb Kalmbach and Heather Kopp

Recovery from Codependency: 6 Studies for Groups or Individuals by Dale and Juanita Ryan (the majority of recovery resources are available on the NACR website)

Memoirs and other books

We've found that reading personal stories about addiction and recovery give us further insight into addiction experiences that are different from ours. We highly recommend reading secular memoirs about recovery from drug addiction, but note that many of them have strong language.

Even in Our Darkness by Jack Deere

Beautiful Boy by David Sheff

Recovery by Russell Brand (lots of language)

The Big Fix by Tracey Helton Mitchell

C. Finding a Counselor

There are different schools of thought when it comes to counseling. And you may need to visit a few before you find the right fit for you. If you are concerned about finding a licensed professional, the Psychology Today database is a great resource. You can search by issue, faith, proximity, insurance, etc. https://www.psychology today.com/us/therapists.

D. Practical Help for Families in Crisis

Often families experiencing devastating loss can't narrow their needs down to a convenient list. There's so much they need, it's overwhelming. In the context of recovery, especially of head of household, the financial hits of addiction and rehab can leave a family struggling for years. Many people are embarrassed and ashamed to ask for help. In these circumstances, anonymous gifts may break down barriers. Some families, however, do come to the church seeking help. Caring for each other is part of our work as the body of Christ.

It's important to remember that while local services like food banks, housing resource centers, and low-income programs are available, not everyone who needs or qualifies for these services is able to obtain them. Whether it's a shortage of resources like housing or a felony drug conviction that inhibits a job search, the obstacles in the way complicate life recovery.

Here are some tangible ways to help, from simple onetime actions to starting programs:

- Drop off groceries anonymously
- Fix their car
- Hire them or help them find work
- Become a licensed childcare
- Establish a counseling fund (they may not want to go to counseling at your church for privacy concerns)
- Pay for activities anonymously (piano lessons, soccer fees, etc.)
- Provide transportation
- Pay for utilities
- Give gift cards for gas

In addition, here is a list of information that can help you or your church point someone in the right direction for help:

- Keep a list available of community resources—food banks, free dinners, free counselors, housing resources, low-cost medical, and if your church is large, who to contact when there is a need.

- In any area of the United States, if you dial 211, or go to 211.org, you will be connected to local resources to help with your needs.

- Rehab—in some situations, addicts qualify for state-funded rehab. Do some research, including checking out the websites above and *Inside Rehab* by Anne M. Fletcher. Also, check out the Citygate Network (www.citygatenet work.org), formerly Association of Gospel Rescue Missions (AGRM.org), for long-term recovery programs.

- Post-rehab—does your community have transitional housing and resources for individuals and families?

- Debt counseling—American Financial Solutions, Christian Financial Counseling. Have some of these resources on hand for your church.

- The phone numbers of a few trusted counselors in your community.

E. The 12 Steps

The 12 Steps were written by Bill W. and became the foundation for Alcoholics Anonymous. They have been adapted for many different addiction support groups, including Christian 12 Step groups, like Celebrate Recovery, that include Scripture references with each step. You can find the full list at www.aa.org.

F. Jellinek Curve

https://www.in.gov/judiciary/ijlap/files/jellinek.pdf.

A Tentative Chart of Alcohol Addiction and Recovery

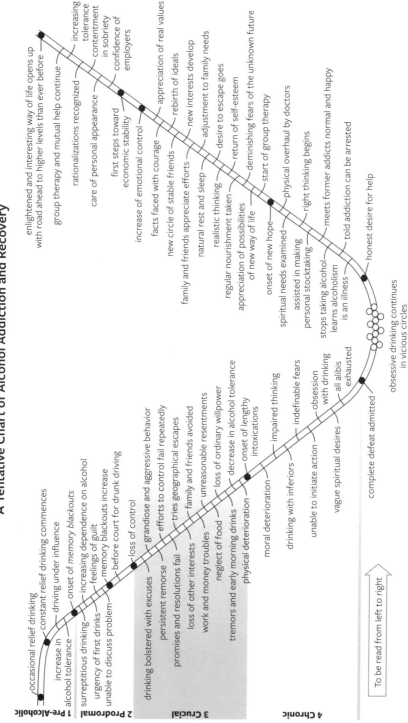

1 Pre-Alcoholic
- occasional relief drinking
- increase in alcohol tolerance
- constant relief drinking commences
- driving under influence
- onset of memory blackouts

2 Prodromal
- surreptitious drinking
- urgency of first drinks
- increasing dependence on alcohol
- feelings of guilt
- memory blackouts increase
- unable to discuss problem
- before court for drunk driving
- loss of control

3 Crucial
- drinking bolstered with excuses
- grandiose and aggressive behavior
- persistent remorse
- efforts to control fail repeatedly
- promises and resolutions fail
- tries geographical escapes
- loss of other interests
- family and friends avoided
- work and money troubles
- unreasonable resentments
- neglect of food
- loss of ordinary willpower
- tremors and early morning drinks
- decrease in alcohol tolerance
- physical deterioration
- onset of lengthy intoxications
- moral deterioration
- impaired thinking
- drinking with inferiors
- indefinable fears
- unable to initiate action
- obsession with drinking
- vague spiritual desires
- all alibis exhausted
- complete defeat admitted

4 Chronic
- obsessive drinking continues in vicious circles
- honest desire for help
- told addiction can be arrested
- learns alcoholism is an illness
- stops taking alcohol
- meets former addicts normal and happy
- right thinking begins
- personal stocktaking
- physical overhaul by doctors
- assisted in making spiritual needs examined
- start of group therapy
- onset of new hope
- appreciation of possibilities of new way of life
- regular nourishment taken
- realistic thinking
- diminishing fears of the unknown future
- natural rest and sleep
- desire to escape goes
- return of self-esteem
- family and friends appreciate efforts
- adjustment to family needs
- new circle of stable friends
- new interests develop
- facts faced with courage
- rebirth of ideals
- increase of emotional control
- appreciation of real values
- economic stability
- first steps toward care of personal appearance
- rationalizations recognized
- contentment in sobriety
- group therapy and mutual help continue
- confidence of employers
- increasing tolerance
- enlightened and interesting way of life opens up with road ahead to higher levels than ever before

To be read from left to right

G. Notes about Struggling with Addiction While in the Ministry

Church ministry is a rough place to battle an addiction. Aside from the fact that living in deception damages our effectiveness and undermines the trust of the people we serve, we are also doing long-term damage to ourselves and our families. Give yourself space to learn how to care for yourself in a healthy way, rather than trying to care for yourself and maintain a front. Whether recovery requires a sabbatical, a leave of absence, or a long break, taking the time to heal properly will help you stay clean long term.

In our experience, stepping away from ministry to heal doesn't have to mean forever. But we believe it's unwise to rush back into leadership and ministry. If your denomination determines your addiction to drugs or alcohol disqualifies you permanently, and you fear this, look around at the incredible ways God is using recovering addicts to minister to people and give them hope. As painful as it is to separate from a denomination you love, watch for how God wants to work in you and through you.

For us, the only way we were ever going to return to ministry was if the church or ministry we were involved in wanted us because of our experience with addiction. Being transparent lessens the temptation to try to keep up the image again. Dave was asked to be a pastor in our church after seven years of sobriety and faithful service.

If you need guidance and prayer, you can find recovery resources for pastors through Celebrate Recovery and the other organizations listed in this appendix. And, if you need someone to talk to who has been through it, send me an email: **Dave at beddoedave@ gmail.com.**

Notes

Introduction

1. Matthew 18:22 NASB.

Chapter 1 Shame Buries Us

1. Substance Abuse and Mental Health Services Administration, *Key Substance Use and Mental Health Indicators in the United States: Results from the 2016 National Survey on Drug Use and Health* (Rockville, MD: Center for Behavioral Health Statistics and Quality, Substance Abuse and Mental Health Services Administration, 2017), https://www.samhsa.gov/data/sites/default/files/NSDUH-FFR1-2016/NSDUH-FFR1-2016.htm.

2. Josh Katz, "Drug Deaths in America Are Rising Faster Than Ever," *New York Times*, June 5, 2017, https://www.nytimes.com/interactive/2017/06/05/upshot/opioid-epidemic-drug-overdose-deaths-are-rising-faster-than-ever.html.

3. Dan Munro, "Inside the $35 Billion Addiction Treatment Industry," *Forbes*, April 27, 2015, https://www.forbes.com/sites/danmunro/2015/04/27/inside-the-35-billion-addiction-treatment-industry/#3218ddf317dc.

4. Alan Meisel, "Pharmacists, Physician-Assisted Suicide, and Pain Control," *Journal of Health Care Law and Policy* 2, no. 2 (1/1999): 211–42, http://digitalcommons.law.umaryland.edu/cgi/viewcontent.cgi?article=1035&context=jhclp.

5. "Do Not Suffer This 'Pain Relief' Bill," *LA Times*, April 26, 2000, http://articles.latimes.com/2000/apr/26/local/me-23711.

6. Frank Brennan, "The US Congressional 'Decade on Pain Control and Research' 2001–2011: A Review," *Journal of Pain & Palliative Care Pharmacotherapy*, 29, no. 3 (2015): 212–27, https://doi.org/10.3109/15360288.2015.1047553.

7. Erik MacLaren, "Is Tramadol the New OxyContin?" DrugAbuse.com, March 21, 2016, https://drugabuse.com/library/is-tramadol-addictive/.

8. Brian F. Mandell, "The Fifth Vital Sign: A Complex Story of Politics and Patient Care," *Cleveland Clinic Journal of Medicine* 83, no. 6 (June 2016): 400–401.

9. Jeremy A. Greene and David Herzberg, "Hidden in Plain Sight: Marketing Prescription Drugs to Consumers in the Twentieth Century," *American Journal of Public Health* 100, no. 5 (2010): 793–803.

10. Mandell, "Fifth Vital Sign," 400–401.

11. "Opioid Painkiller Prescribing: Where You Live Makes a Difference," Centers for Disease Control and Prevention, July 2014, https://www.cdc.gov/vitalsigns/opioid-prescribing/index.html.

12. "Opioid Painkiller Prescribing."

13. "Prescription Opioid Data," Centers for Disease Control and Prevention, December 19, 2018, https://www.cdc.gov/drugoverdose/data/prescribing.html.

14. The Drug Enforcement Administration (DEA) reclassified Tramadol to a controlled substance in 2014 because of the danger of addiction, potential for overdose, and severity of withdrawal.

15. This was 1998. Tramadol was not closely regulated until 2014.

16. Omar Manejwala, "How Often Do Long-Term Sober Alcoholics and Addicts Relapse?" *Psychology Today*, February 13, 2016, https://www.psychologytoday.com/us/blog/craving/201402/how-often-do-long-term-sober-alcoholics-and-addicts-relapse.

According to an eight-year study on the relationship of the duration of sobriety to recovery, the longer a person breaking free from addiction can stay clean and sober, the more likely their chance of successful recovery, so those days are critical.

17. Proverbs 14:1.

18. John 11:4.

19. John 11:44 NASB.

20. Charles Haddon Spurgeon, "Unbinding Lazarus" (sermon no. 1776, Metropolitan Tabernacle, London, April 20, 1884), http://www.spurgeongems.org/vols28–30/chs1776.pdf.

21. Spurgeon, "Unbinding Lazarus."

Chapter 2 Reviving Compassion

1. Tracey Helton Mitchell, *The Big Fix: Hope after Heroin* (Berkeley: Seal, 2016), 17.

2. Rajita Sinha, "New Findings on Biological Factors Predicting Addiction Relapse Vulnerability," *Current Psychiatry Reports* 13, no. 5 (October 2011): 398–405.

3. Anne M. Fletcher, *Inside Rehab: The Surprising Truth about Addiction Treatment—and How to Get Help That Works* (New York: Viking Penguin, 2013), 93.

4. Melody Beattie, *Codependent No More: How to Stop Controlling Others and Start Caring for Yourself*, 2nd ed. (Center City, MN: Hazelden, 1992), 36.

5. Beverly Engel, "How Compassion Can Help You Support an Addicted Loved One," *Psychology Today*, October 3, 2016, https://www.psychologytoday.com/us/blog/the-compassion-chronicles/201610/how-compassion-can-help-you-support-addicted-loved-one.

6. Dale Ryan and Juanita Ryan, Recovery from *Codependency* (Richmond, VA: NACR, 1992), 1, https://www.nacr.org/nacr-store/bible-studies-by-dale-and-juanita-ryan.

7. Christopher Kennedy Lawford and Beverly Engel, *When Your Partner Has an Addiction: How Compassion Can Transform Your Relationship (and Heal You Both in the Process)* (Dallas: BenBella, 2016), 102.

8. Jack Deere, *Even in Our Darkness: A Story of Beauty in a Broken Life* (Grand Rapids: Zondervan, 2018), 265–66.

9. Sinha, "New Findings on Biological Factors," 398–405.

10. Johann Hari, "Everything You Think You Know about Addiction Is Wrong," TED video, TEDGlobalLondon, June 2015, 14:42, https://www.ted.com /talks/johann_hari_everything_you_think_you_know_about_addiction_is _wrong?language=en.

11. Psychology Today Glossary, "empathy," https://www.psychologytoday .com/us/basics/empathy.

12. Hebrews 4:15.

13. Brennan Manning, *The Ragamuffin Gospel: Good News for the Bedraggled, Beat-Up, and Burnt Out* (Portland: Multnomah, 1990), 147.

14. Lawford and Engel, *When Your Partner Has an Addiction*, 39.

15. Lawford and Engel, 40.

16. Psalm 145:8.

17. Romans 2:4.

18. 1 John 4:19.

Chapter 3 A Marriage in Recovery

1. Anonymous, A Marriage in Recovery, *The Guardian*, https://www.theguard ian.com/lifeandstyle/series/a-marriage-in-recovery.

2. Anonymous, "I Tried to Stop My Husband Drinking," A Marriage in Recovery, *The Guardian*, May 18, 2013, https://www.theguardian.com/lifeandstyle /2013/may/18/stop-husband-drinking.

3. Anonymous, "R Is Four Months Sober," Marriage in Recovery, May 25, 2013, https://www.theguardian.com/lifeandstyle/2013/may/25/four-months-sober -after-rehab (emphasis added).

4. Anonymous, "The Hardest Thing about Living with an Alcoholic Is Not Knowing If—or When—He Will Drink Again," Marriage in Recovery, February 15, 2014, https://www.theguardian.com/lifeandstyle/2014/feb/15/hardest-thing -alcoholic-not-knowing.

5. Luke 17:3–4.

6. 1 Corinthians 13:4–7.

7. Brené Brown, *The Gifts of Imperfection: Let Go of Who You Think You're Supposed to Be and Embrace Who You Are* (Center City, MN: Hazelden, 2010), 40.

8. Harriet Lerner, *The Dance of Anger: A Woman's Guide to Changing the Patterns of Intimate Relationships* (New York: William Morrow, 2014), 57.

9. John 8.

10. John Ortberg, *Everybody's Normal Till You Get to Know Them* (Grand Rapids: Zondervan, 2003), 95.

11. Brené Brown, *Rising Strong: The Reckoning. The Rumble. The Revolution.* (New York: Spiegel & Grau, 2015), 150.

12. C. S. Lewis, *The Four Loves: An Exploration of the Nature of Love* (New York: Houghton Mifflin Harcourt, 1960), 122.

13. Søren Kierkegaard, "Under the Spell of Good Intentions," in *Provocations: Spiritual Writings of Kierkegaard*, ed. Charles E. Moore (Farmington, PA: The Bruderhof Foundation, 2002), 14. Reprinted from www.bruderhof.com. Copyright 2002 by The Bruderhof Foundation, Inc. Used with permission. http://www.ldo lphin.org/Provocations.pdf.

Chapter 4 The Support of Family

1. Generations United, *Raising the Children of the Opioid Epidemic: Solutions and Support for Grandfamilies*, State of Grandfamilies in America Annual Report 2016, https://www.gu.org/app/uploads/2018/05/Grandfamilies-Report -SOGF-2016.pdf.

2. Luke 15:20 NLT.

3. John 6:37.

4. Stephen Arterburn and David Stoop, *Understanding and Loving a Person with Alcohol or Drug Addiction* (Colorado Springs: David C. Cook, 2018), 34.

5. J. Keith Miller, *A Hunger for Healing: The Twelve Steps as a Classic Model for Christian Spiritual Growth* (New York: HarperCollins, 1991), 4.

6. Vincent J. Felitti et al., "Relationship of Childhood Abuse and Household Dysfunction to Many of the Leading Causes of Death in Adults," *American Journal of Preventive Medicine* 14, no. 4 (May 1998): 245–58, https://www.cdc .gov/violenceprevention/acestudy/about.html.

7. Jeremiah 6:14 TLB.

8. Jacqueline Howard, "Thailand Cave Rescue: The Health Toll of Waiting for Freedom," CNN, July 5, 2018, https://www.cnn.com/2018/07/03/health/cave -rescue-psychological-toll-explainer/index.html.

9. Center for Substance Abuse Treatment, "Chapter 1: Substance Abuse Treatment and Family Therapy," in *Substance Abuse Treatment and Family Therapy*, Treatment Improvement Protocol (TIP) Series, no. 39 (Rockville, MD: Substance Abuse and Mental Health Services Administration, 2004), https://www.ncbi.nlm .nih.gov/books/NBK64269/.

Chapter 5 Friendship in Recovery

1. John 15:13.

2. 2 Corinthians 2:7.

3. Proverbs 19:11 BSB.

4. Christine D. Pohl, *Living into Community: Cultivating Practices That Sustain Us* (Grand Rapids: Eerdmans, 2012), 132.

5. Substance Abuse and Mental Health Services Administration, *Key Substance Use and Mental Health Indicators*.

6. Bruce Schreiner, "Feds: Descent to Addiction Often Starts at Home," Associated Press, April 25, 2012, http://archive.boston.com/lifestyle/health/articles /2012/04/25/feds_descent_to_addiction_often_starts_at_home/.

7. Romans 14:20.

8. Mitchell, *The Big Fix*, 104–6.

9. Ryan, *Recovery from Bitterness*, 1.

10. 1 Peter 4:8.

11. "About the CDC-Kaiser ACE Study," Centers for Disease Control and Prevention, June 14, 2016, https://www.cdc.gov/violenceprevention/childabuse andneglect/acestudy/about.html.

12. Job 1:21.

13. Job 2:13.

14. Colossians 3:13 NLT.

Chapter 6 The Mission of the Church

1. John Gramlich, "Nearly Half of Americans Have a Family Member or Close Friend Who's Been Addicted to Drugs," Pew Research Center, October 26, 2017, http://www.pewresearch.org/fact-tank/2017/10/26/nearly-half-of-americans-have -a-family-member-or-close-friend-whos-been-addicted-to-drugs/.

2. Substance Abuse and Mental Health Services Administration, *Key Substance Use and Mental Health Indicators*.

3. Dietrich Bonhoeffer, *Life Together: The Classic Exploration of Faith in Community* (New York: Harper & Row, 1954), 110.

4. Manning, *Ragamuffin Gospel*, 28.

5. James 1:4 CSB.

6. Jonathan Benz and Kristina Robb-Dover, *The Recovery-Minded Church: Loving and Ministering to People with Addiction* (Downers Grove, IL: InterVarsity, 2016), 15.

7. Benz and Robb-Dover, *The Recovery-Minded Church*, 31.

8. Liz Swanson and Teresa McBean, *Bridges to Grace: Innovative Approaches to Recovery Ministry* (Grand Rapids: Zondervan, 2011), 5.

9. Kathleen Norris, *Dakota: A Spiritual Geography* (New York: Houghton Mifflin, 1993), 130.

10. Swanson and McBean, *Bridges to Grace*, 30.

11. Swanson and McBean, *Bridges to Grace*, 29.

12. Substance Abuse and Mental Health Services Administration, "Co-occurring Disorders," March 8, 2016, https://www.samhsa.gov/disorders/co-occurring.

13. Bonhoeffer, *Life Together*, 97.

14. James 1:19.

15. Douglas Bursch, *The Community of God: A Theology of the Church from a Reluctant Pastor* (Seattle: Fairly Spiritual, 2017), 196–97.

16. Sky Jethani, *Immeasurable: Reflections on the Soul of Ministry in the Age of Church, Inc.* (Chicago: Moody, 2017), 210.

17. 1 Corinthians 6:11 NKJV.

18. Matthew 6:3–4.

19. Dale S. Ryan, "Recovery Ministry in the Local Church," Center for Recovery Ministry in the Local Church, The National Association for Christian Recovery, 2019, https://www.nacr.org/center-for-recovery-at-church/recovery -ministry-in-the-local-church-2.

20. Romans 5–6.

21. Manning, *Ragamuffin Gospel*, 156.

22. Isaiah 53:3.

Chapter 7 The Power of a Support Group

1. It's important to separate conscience and conviction from the sort of shame we're addressing here. Shame makes you believe you are alone and that no one could possibly be as bad as you, as in you are both unlovable and unforgivable. Shame causes you to hide behind a mask and not let anyone see or know what you're struggling with because you fear rejection.

2. David Sheff, *Beautiful Boy: A Father's Journey through His Son's Addiction* (New York: Houghton Mifflin, 2008), 173–74.

3. Reinhold Niebuhr, "The Serenity Prayer."

4. Job 38:2 NASB.

5. Philippians 3:13 NASB.

6. 1 Corinthians 6:11 NASB.

7. 2 Corinthians 1:4.

Chapter 8 The Healing Effect of Counseling

1. "Addiction," *Nova*, PBS, October 17, 2018, 38:23, https://www.pbs.org/wgbh/nova/video/addiction.

2. Jane Ellen Stevens, "Addiction Doc Says: It's Not the Drugs. It's the ACEs . . . Adverse Childhood Experiences," Aces Too High, (May 2, 2017), https://acestoohigh.com/2017/05/02/addiction-doc-says-stop-chasing-the-drug-focus-on-aces-people-can-recover/.

3. "About the CDC-Kaiser ACE Study."

4. Miller, *A Hunger for Healing*, 4.

5. Beattie, *Codependent No More*, 153.

6. J. D. Vance, *Hillbilly Elegy: A Memoir of a Family and Culture in Crisis* (New York: HarperCollins, 2016), 228.

Chapter 9 The Role of Rehab

1. Nora D. Volkow, *Principles of Drug Addiction Treatment: A Research-Based Guide (Third Edition)*, National Institute on Drug Abuse, January 2018, https://www.drugabuse.gov/node/pdf/675/principles-of-drug-addiction-treatment-a-research-based-guide-third-edition.

2. Barbara Weiner, "Rich Histories Merge: Meet the New Hazelden-Betty Ford Foundation," *SALIS Journal* 1 (2014): 84, http://salis.org/salisjournal/vol1/vol1_2014.pdf.

3. David Sheff, "Viewpoint: We Need to Rethink Rehab," *Time*, April 3, 2013, http://ideas.time.com/2013/04/03/we-need-to-rethink-rehab/.

4. William White, quoted in Fletcher, *Inside Rehab*, 393.

5. Fletcher, *Inside Rehab*, 394.

Chapter 10 The Safety Net of Social Services

1. The White House, "The Underestimated Cost of the Opioid Crisis," The Council of Economic Advisers, November 2017, 1, https://www.whitehouse.gov/sites/whitehouse.gov/files/images/The%20Underestimated%20Cost%20of%20the%20Opioid%20Crisis.pdf.

2. Emily Birnbaum and Maya Lora, "Opioid Crisis Sending Thousands of Children into Foster Care," *The Hill*, June 20, 2018, https://thehill.com/policy/healthcare/393129-opioid-crisis-sending-thousands-of-children-into-foster-care.

3. "21.3 Percent of U.S. Population Participates in Government Assistance Programs Each Month," United States Census Bureau, release no. CB15-97, May 28, 2015,
https://www.census.gov/newsroom/press-releases/2015/cb15-97.html.

4. "State Fact Sheets: How States Have Spent Funds under the TANF Block Grant," Center on Budget and Policy Priorities, updated February 19, 2019, https://www.cbpp.org/research/family-income-support/state-fact-sheets-how-states-have-spent-funds-under-the-tanf-block.

5. *The Missionary Register for M DCCC XX* (London: L. B. Seeley, 1820), 466, https://books.google.com/books?id=qoxQAQAAMAAJ&printsec=frontcover#v=onepage&q&f=false.

6. 1 John 3:17.

Chapter 11 Advocacy for Medical Care

1. Mitchell, *The Big Fix*, 156–57.

2. Jessie's Law, S. 581, 115th Congr. (2017), https://www.congress.gov/bill/115th-congress/senate-bill/581.

3. "Opioid Overdose Crisis," National Institute on Drug Abuse, January 2019, https://www.drugabuse.gov/drugs-abuse/opioids/opioid-overdose-crisis.

4. Claudia Wallis, "Why We Won't Miss Opioids," *Scientific American*, June 1, 2018, https://scientificamerican.com/article/why-we-wont-miss-opioids/?am#.

5. Dr. Aditi Vyas, "Opioids after Wisdom Teeth Removal Might Set Young People Up for Addiction," ABC News, August 7, 2018, https://abcnews.go.com/Health/opioids-wisdom-teeth-removal-set-young-people-addiction/story?id=57081387.

6. "Addiction Medicine: Closing the Gap between Science and Practice," Center on Addiction, June 2012, https://www.centeronaddiction.org/addiction-research/reports/addiction-medicine-closing-gap-between-science-and-practice.

7. "American Dental Association Announces New Policy to Combat Opioid Epidemic," American Dental Association, March 26, 2018, https://www.ada.org/en/press-room/news-releases/2018-archives/march/american-dental-association-announces-new-policy-to-combat-opioid-epidemic.

8. Sarah Larney and Michael Farrell, "Yes, People Can Die from Opiate Withdrawal," *Addiction* 112, no. 2 (February 2017): 199–200, https://onlinelibrary.wiley.com/doi/full/10.1111/add.13512.

Chapter 12 A Restorer of Homes

1. See 1 Peter 2:24; Luke 9:23.
2. John 12:11 BSB.
3. Flannery O'Connor, *The Habit of Being: Letters of Flannery O'Connor*, ed. Sally Fitzgerald (New York: Farrar, Straus & Giroux, 1979), 307.
4. Job 2:9.
5. 1 Corinthians 10:12–13 ESV.
6. Henri J. M. Nouwen, *The Inner Voice of Love: A Journey through Anguish to Freedom* (New York: Doubleday, 1996), 7.

Deborah Beddoe has been a writer for numerous nonprofit recovery ministries including rescue missions and Prison Fellowship. **David Beddoe**, now a pastor, has worked in recovery ministry for nearly a decade following his own fifteen-year battle with prescription drug addiction. Their story has been featured in *Guideposts* and *Christianity Today*. The Beddoes have four grown and nearly grown children and live in the Pacific Northwest.

DeborahBeddoe.com

Listen to *Deb and Dave's* podcast, *We Digress*, on Spotify or your favorite podcast app.

 DebandDaveBeddoe